# SOLUTIONS FOR BLACK AMERICA

*by*

Jawanza Kunjufu

African American Images
CHICAGO

Front cover design by Harold Carr
Copyright © 2004 by Jawanza Kunjufu
First edition, second printing

Printed in the United States of America

ISBN: 0-913543-98-5

# DEDICATION

This book is dedicated to the million African American families who live in squalor and poverty and who earn less than $7,000 annually. How can this happen in the richest country in the world? I also dedicate this book to the 20 percent of African American adults who earn less than $14,000 per year and, unfortunately, the 50 percent of African American children who live in their households.

Who holds the agenda for them? Do DuBois' talented tenth and the Black middle class have the agenda for them? Has integration improved the plight of this population? Have affirmative action and the Great Society improved the living conditions for this population? Have the almost 10,000 African American elected officials, many of them mayors, improved the living conditions of these citizens? Albeit, I wrote this book primarily for "the least of these."

# CONTENTS

I thank God for my wife, two sons, and grandson.

I have prayed to my Lord and Savior Jesus Christ for Him to use my mind throughout this book. I have prayed to the Holy Spirit to fill me with His power. I pray that you, the reader, will be more than just a hearer of these words, but a doer also. I am confident because of the scriptures that God's word will not come back void, but will accomplish that for which it was sent out. To God be the Glory.

# QUESTIONS

1. Why do we spend more time talking about the problem than working on the solution?
2. What is the agenda for Black America?
3. Are Black leaders reactionary and respond only to crisis?
4. Are Black leaders proactive?
5. What percentage of African Americans benefited from integration?
6. Can the Black family and community survive if one-third of its men are involved with the penal institution?
7. What has been the progress of the Black poor over the past 50 years?
8. If racism ended tonight, would it increase African Americans' test scores? Would it increase Black consumer support of Black businesses? Would it decrease crime, divorce, STDs, teen pregnancy, and fatherlessness?
9. Are African Americans suffering from post-traumatic slavery disorder?
10. Does the Democratic Party treat African Americans like a mistress?
11. What is the role of the Black church in the liberation struggle?
12. What percentage of Black resources should be allocated to marching?
13. What percentage of Black resources should be allocated to community development?
14. What advice would Harriet Tubman, Martin Delaney, Fredrick Douglass, Booker T. Washington, W.E.B. Dubois, Marcus Garvey, Martin Luther King, Jr., Fanny Lou Hamer, and Malcolm X offer us in this new millennium?
15. How do we improve the communication between civil rights activists and the hip hop community?

# INTRODUCTION

I have been blessed with many mentors, and one of them is Dr. Barbara Sizemore, the brilliant educator who taught me over two decades ago the following theoretical paradigm:

## Problem    Cause    Solution    Implementation

This book uses this theoretical paradigm. When I speak, especially to schools, I use this paradigm. In the typical one-hour workshop, speakers will use 55 minutes to talk about the problem, 4 minutes to discuss the cause, 1 minute to suggest a solution, and we'll come back next year to talk about implementation. You would think, after all these national conferences, symposiums, and state-of-the-race discussions that we would be much further advanced in regard to solutions and implementation.

In the "Economics" chapter, we will look at myriad issues. One of them is, Why do our largest 150 Black organizations spend $16 billion annually in White hotels using White airlines to talk about what the White man is doing to them? Masters Hilton, Hyatt, and Marriott and Delta, American, and United airlines I'm sure are saying, "Talk about me as long as you want. Just please do not stop spending $16 billion with me."

For some reason, we are obsessed with talking about the problem. In low-achieving schools, the most negative room is not where the students are, it is the teachers' lounge. In this room, teachers love talking about the problem. If you want to hear about the problem, all you need to do is go to the barbershop, beauty shop, nail salon, or lounge in any Black community.

I am a frequent guest on radio and television talk shows, and it amazes me how much the public really likes talking about the problems. If I am on a show discussing my book *Countering the Conspiracy to Destroy Black Boys*, the operative word "conspiracy" fuels the discussion, and the talk show host wants to keep me on forever because of the tremendous volume of callers who want to talk about conspiracy theories, racism, and White supremacy. When I am on a show discussing my book *Developing Positive Self-Images and Discipline in Black Children* or *Black Economics*, I have to do the majority of the talking because the callers are absent.

It reminds me of the larger media that have the philosophy, "If it bleeds, it leads." The media's assumption is that stories involving violence and negativity attract a larger audience. I'd personally rather watch shows about how Pastor James Meeks at Salem Baptist Church in Chicago closed down liquor stores and turned a neighborhood dry or how MAD DADS is patrolling streets and reducing crime. I want to know more about Rev. Eugene Rivers and the 10-Point Boston Miracle or about the great work Joseph Marshall is doing in San Francisco with the Omega Boys Club. In the last chapter, "Implementation/Models of Success," we'll look at these and much more in detail.

It's one thing for the media to take the position that if it bleeds it leads. But it's very disappointing when the African American media and its audience take the same approach. A very good friend of mine, Bob Law, who was the talk show host for the nationally syndicated show "Night Talk," became so frustrated with people talking about the problem that he used a classic word to quench that train of thought. He would first listen to the callers talk about the problem. Many times they would go on for numerous minutes. Finally, Bob would say, "Therefore?" The caller would be taken aback and not understand what Bob was asking. Bob, in his own unique way, would explain: "Now that we've heard your diatribe on the problem, can you, therefore, tell us what we should do about it?" There would be moments of silence.

It reminds me of Robert Woodson's challenge to Black leadership. He says, "How is it that Black leaders know the problem, talk about the problem, make money off the problem, but can't solve the problem?"[1]

When Dr. Sizemore was teaching me this paradigm, she cautioned me: "Never give a group your solution until there's a consensus on what caused the problem." She explained to me that if you're speaking to a group of teachers and it's agreed that the problem is the achievement gap between Black and White students, it would be futile to offer your solutions without hearing what they thought caused the problem.

For example, if educators believe the reason for the 200-point gap between African American and White students on the SAT is because the Black children come from low-income, single parent homes, then offering them solutions of raising student expectations and requiring students to spend greater time on task would not address their causes.

Throughout this book, we will parallel causes and solutions. We first have to come to a consensus on what caused the problem. Then and only then will we be in a position to offer the appropriate solution and, hopefully, inspire its implementation.

In this book the first two chapters are entitled "Problems" and "Causes," respectively. The third chapter is "Integration Revisited." I've often thought about Montgomery, Alabama, 1955, and the 381 days that we shut Montgomery down in that historic bus strike. Hindsight is always 20/20. Now we must ask ourselves, Has integration been good for the least of these? We know it's been very good for the one-third of African Americans who earn more than $50,000 per year, but what about the 20 percent of the African American community that lives below the poverty line?

The chapter after that is "Education." We will raise the question, Is the future of the Black race in the hands of White female teachers? Another very significant issue is the debate in the African American community about vouchers. It concerns me that Black leadership, which is supposed to represent its constituency, is not in favor of choice, although they send their children to private schools. There have been numerous polls and studies showing that the majority of low-income African American parents who cannot afford tuition favor vouchers and school choice.

The following chapter is "Family and Health." Of all the factors that we will look at in that chapter, I believe the most significant one is fatherlessness. How can the African American family grow and develop if only 32 percent of its children are blessed with a father who stays in the home? If racism ended tonight, would it reduce the number of sperm donors in the Black community?

The subsequent chapter is "Economics." I really believe that if African Americans spent more than the current 4 percent of their collective $688 billion with each other, we could solve the majority of our problems. It has been said that we would have to go back to Jim Crow and segregation to increase that 4 percent to 20 percent. I appeal to everyone reading this book to examine their checkbook, review their budget, and sincerely ask themselves, What can I do to increase my expenditures with African American businesses? We could tremendously reduce our 12 percent adult unemployment rate and 37 percent youth unemployment rate if we simply acted and operated like Asians, Arabs, and Jews.

The next chapter is "Politics and Organizing." Al Sharpton raised a profound question when he asked, "Does the Democratic Party treat us like a mistress?" In the 2000 election, 95 percent of the African American vote went to Al Gore; yet, the Democratic Party did not construct one agenda item for the African American community. We will also look into the significance of organizing and political movements. How did Marcus Garvey in 1920 organize over one million African Americans without a cell phone, fax machine, television, or the Internet?

In the chapter "Post-Traumatic Slavery Disorder/ Africentricity," we will show that just as Montgomery 1955 was pivotal in Black history, so was 1865. Just as psychologists were deployed to Columbine and Oklahoma City and other disaster areas in this country, the same effort should have been made for African Americans when slavery officially ended with the 13th Amendment in 1865. Abraham Lincoln's Emancipation Proclamation of 1863 did not free anyone. Every African American should have received counseling from an Africentric psychologist, counselor, or pastor. I sincerely believe that we will be free only when we believe that Whoopi Goldberg looks as good as Halle Berry and that Jesus Christ looks like us.

The following chapter is the "Black Church." Originally, I had put my discussion of the church into the "Implementation/ Models of Success" chapter, but when you have 85,000 churches with more than 16 million members, receiving $3 billion annually and holding $50 billion in assets, I think you'd agree that the Black church needs an exclusive chapter.

The final chapter is "Implementation/Models of Success." How can a people who earn $688 billion annually, possess four million college graduates, and elect almost 10,000 government officials have so little power? Is it lack of unity, ignorance, fear, lack of work, lack of economic support? Why have we not moved from theory to practice?

In closing, just as I strongly agree with Bob Law and Robert Woodson, the guiding light for me is my Lord and Savior Jesus Christ. In Genesis 1, when it was dark, God said, "Let there be light." He didn't dwell on the problem. He didn't talk about how dark it was. He said, "Let there be light." This book is about shedding light.

# CHAPTER 1

# PROBLEMS

One of three African American males
is involved in the penal institution.
It is projected that by 2020,
two of three African American males
will be involved.

Twenty percent of African American adults
and 50 percent of African American children
live below the poverty line.
Forty percent of the homeless
are African Americans.

# Problems

Only 6 percent of White adults
are unemployed,
but 12 percent of African American adults
are unemployed.
Only 15 percent of White youth
are unemployed,
but 37 percent of African American youth
are unemployed.
Forty percent of Black males ages 16-65
are unemployed.

America has lost three million middle class,
health insurance paying, manufacturing jobs.
It has had the greatest impact
on African Americans due to
last hired-first fired discrimination.
In addition, African Americans are least able
educationally to compete in this
high-technological economy.
New York lost 520,000, Chicago 326,000,
Philadelphia 160,000 and Detroit 108,000.
These jobs cannot be replaced with lower
class jobs that do not pay health insurance.
Seventy-five percent of new economy jobs
are in the service sector which include
security, health aides, waitressing,
janitorial, and cashiering.

# Problems

Black median income is $32,000
versus White median income of $45,000.
Black per capita wealth is $10,000
versus White per capita wealth of $55,000.
One percent of the population
owns 48% of the wealth.
Ten percent of the population
owns 86% of the wealth.

Median SAT scores:

| | |
|---|---|
| Asians | 1083 |
| Whites | 1063 |
| Hispanics | 903 |
| African Americans | 857 |

# Problems

African Americans constitute
12 percent of the population,
but African American males account for
43 percent of HIV cases;
and African American women are
64 percent.

In 14 of 16 health categories—diabetes, hypertension, heart disease, stroke, cancer, infant mortality, etc.—African Americans sufferers outnumber Whites.

# Problems

Only 32 percent of African American children
have fathers in the home.
The divorce rate in Black America
is 66 percent.

In Los Angeles, African Americans
constitute 11 percent of the population,
but represent 47 percent of the murder victims.
In Washington, DC, 1 of every 12
African American males die of homicide.

# Problems

Among African American male
high school students:
One in 200,000 will play in the NBA.
One in 3,700 will earn a Ph.D.
One in 766 will become a lawyer.
One in 395 will become a doctor.
One in 195 will become a teacher.
One in 20 will be incarcerated.
One in 12 will have an STD.
One in 9 will use cocaine.
One in 3 will drop out of high school.

There are 36 million "disconnected" youth in America. These youth, 60 percent Black and Hispanic, have
left high school, lack credentials, and are unemployed.[2]

# Problems

The Centers for Disease Control's
National Center for Health Statistics
in a report entitled "Cohabitation, Marriage,
Divorce and Remarriage in the United States,"
showed that Black women are facing a crisis
in their relationships with Black men.
According to this study, when compared to
all other racial groups, Black women are:

Least likely to marry,
Least likely to marry a long-term
cohabiting partner,
Most likely to have their marriages end in
separation or divorce,
Most likely to remain separated or divorced,
Least likely to remarry,
Most likely to see their second marriages end.

# CHAPTER 2

# CAUSES

In Barbara Sizemore's theoretical paradigm, after stating the problem, identifying the cause is the most important factor. Solutions can only be provided when the cause has been established and agreed upon. Unfortunately, one of the major challenges in the African American community, especially among its leadership, is that we cannot collectively agree on the causes. Can you imagine being at a conference of African American leaders that included Jesse Jackson, Sr., Ward Connerly, Al Sharpton, Shelby Steele, Kweisi Mfume, Walter Williams, Louis Farrakhan, and Dinesh D'Souza, with all eight men expressing diverse views?

Walter Williams says, "The major problems that stand in the way of Black advancement will be solved only when Blacks finally recognize that our destinies lie in our hands. Only we can solve what are essentially Black problems— not Washington, politicians, and the intellectual elite."

Jesse Jackson, Sr., says, "The hands that picked cotton now pick presidents. We must demand our fair share. Cut us in or we must cut you out. If I were to compose a four-movement Freedom Symphony, the first movement would be slavery to emancipation. The second was ending legalized segregation. The third would be the Voting Rights Act, and the last movement is the equitable distribution of capital."

Ward Connerly says, "It is high time for those who are obsessed with color to develop a little color blindness. We have to stop dwelling on past injustices like slavery and segregation. We have to accept this fact. We can't use race to get beyond race."

Al Sharpton says, "No Justice, No Peace. Our dignity should never be compromised. We will no longer allow ourselves to be screwed by Democrats or Republicans."

Shelby Steele says, "It is time for those who seek identity and power through grievance groups to fashion identities apart from grievances, to grant themselves the widest range of freedom and assume responsibility for that freedom."

Louis Farrakhan says, "We need separate states and we must do for self. We want an immediate end to police brutality. We demand freedom and justice."

Dinesh D'Souza says, "One thing is clear. Racism is no longer the main problem facing Blacks or any group in America today. Even if racism were to disappear overnight, this would do nothing to improve Black test scores, increase Black entrepreneurs, strengthen Black families, or reduce Black on Black crime. These problems have taken on a cultural existence of their own and need to be confronted on their own terms."

Kweisi Mfume says, "If in fighting for freedom, we relinquish the liberties that are the foundation of our society, we will lose everything for which we have ever fought. America is becoming more multicultural and we support affirmative action."

Listed below is a chart that will further attempt to clarify the divergent views that these camps possess.

| Problems | Causes | |
| --- | --- | --- |
| | **Liberals** | **Conservatives** |
| 1. Overall Condition | Racism | Lack of middle-class values |
| 2. Income | 20% earn less than $14,000 annually | 32% earn greater than $50,000 annually |
| 3. Test Scores | Test Bias, funding inequities | Lack of study time |
| 4. Affirmative Action | Needed | Color blind society, unnecessary crutch |

# Causes

| Problems | Causes | |
|---|---|---|
| | **Liberals** | **Conservatives** |
| 5. Crime | More rehabilitation, change drug sentencing laws | 3 strikes and you're out laws |
| 6. Politics | Democrats | Republicans |
| 7. World View | Collective view | Self-centered |

## Black/White Responses on Operational Issues, Policy Values and Perceptions of Racial Status

### 1. Operational issues
Agree: "It is the responsibility of the federal government to ensure equality with Whites, even if we have to pay more taxes."

| Issue | Black | White | Difference |
|---|---|---|---|
| Jobs | 73% | 40% | 33% |
| Schools | 89% | 65% | 24% |
| Health care | 90% | 55% | 35% |
| Courts and police | 89% | 69% | 20% |

## Average difference = 28%

### 2. Policy values

| Issue | Black | White | Difference |
|---|---|---|---|
| Favor school vouchers | 46% | 44% | 2% |
| Accept same-sex marriages | 29% | 35% | 6% |
| Accept having a child outside marriage | 73% | 60% | 7% |
| Accept felons voting rights | 76% | 58% | 18% |
| Religion most/very important | 80% | 57% | 23% |

## Average difference = 10%

| Issue | Black | White | Difference |
|---|---|---|---|
| Favor trans-racial adoption | 84% | 80% | 4% |
| Race should not be a factor for minorities in securing jobs, education, and so on | 86% | 94% | 8% |
| Favor extra effort to reach out to qualified minorities | 77% | 49% | 28% |
| Favor more minorities in Congress | 75% | 32% | 43% |
| Oppose using race in redistricting | 70% | 90% | 20% |

## Average difference = 20%

## 3. Perceptions of racial status

### *Percentage that agree with statements*

| Issue | Black | White | Difference |
|---|---|---|---|
| Blacks have less opportunity than Whites | 74% | 27% | 47% |
| Lots/some discrimination against African Americans | 86% | 71% | 15% |
| Still major problems facing racial minorities | 88% | 63% | 25% |

## Average difference = 29%

Source: *Washington Post*/Kaiser Family Foundation/Harvard University poll.

# Causes

When you talk to African American leaders or the masses of Black people, the major cause of the plight in the Black community is racism. Ward Connerly says that we need to develop a color blind society. His objective is to abolish race as a factor in census data. On the other hand, D'Souza says racism is no longer the main problem facing Blacks or any other group in America. Sharpton, Mfume, Jackson, and Farrakhan clearly disagree.

I wonder what Ward Connerly and Dinesh D'Souza would have to say about the following research. In the period from July 2001 through May 2002, Marianne Bertrend, an assistant professor of economics at the University of Chicago, and Sendhil Mullainathan, an assistant professor at Massachusetts Institute of Technology, sent 5,000 fictitious resumes in response to more than 1,300 employment ads in the Sunday editions of the Boston Globe and the Chicago Tribune. All of the resumes stated similar or identical credentials, but some respondents had supposedly Black-sounding names, like Lakisha and Jamal, while others possessed White-sounding names, like Emily and Taylor. All the jobs were in sales, customer service, clerical, and administrative support.

Overall, resumes with White names got 50 percent more calls for interviews than those with Black names. To further test the premise, the professors also put Black names on some resumes that listed better skills, and White names on some resumes with lesser skills. When they tabulated their responses, they found Whites with better skills got 30 percent more calls than Whites with lesser skills, but resumes with Black-sounding names that listed higher skills didn't garner appreciably more interest from employers than Black-sounding resumes exhibiting lesser skills.

A study also found that job discrimination is uniform across occupations and industries. Federal contractors and employers who listed "Equal Opportunity Employer" in their ads discriminated as much as any other employers.

A study using names based on data from birth certificates of Blacks and Whites born in Massachusetts found that applicants with White names needed to send about 10 resumes to get one call, but Blacks with African American names needed to send about 15 resumes to get one call. According to the report, a White name yielded as many calls as an additional eight years of experience.[3]

I often drive by construction sites in the Black community and see 10 workers—all White. I see 10 providers, male and female, 10 adults eligible to propose marriage to someone. Their job allows them to buy a house and to ultimately provide for their children. It is very difficult to live in a capitalistic society without capital and/or employment. I think it is very naive and disingenuous for Connerly, D'Souza, Steele, Williams, and others to believe that race is not a factor in American society.

Let me juxtapose the above studies with an experience I had in Florida concerning the FCAT (Florida Comprehensive Assessment Test) and high-stakes testing. Florida, along with many other states, now requires that its students at certain grade levels, normally 3rd, 8th, and 12th, be tested to show mastery at that particular grade level before matriculating to the next grade. I was brought into the state to address the issue. Almost 40,000 children had been retained and a disproportionate number of them were African American. The Black community was split. Some leaders felt that the reasons for the poor African American performance were inferior schools, ineffective teachers, inadequate funding, and test bias.

# Causes

This group was very vocal and created protests and marches that extended from Miami to Tallahassee, the state capital.

On the other hand, I noticed another faction of the Black community that was not as vocal, but felt that African American students needed to study more. How do we explain the fact that so-called inferior schools with inadequate funding and ineffective teachers resulted in 80 percent of the African American students passing the test? How do we explain that Asians and Hispanics often outperform African Americans on tests even though they might have a language barrier? Aren't the tests culturally biased against them?

I was very concerned about leaders using African American youth in the march. My first concern was how the youth felt about participating in the march. Did they feel that they needed African American leaders to protest for them because they could not pass the test? Were they desirous of the leaders to negotiate a deal whereby they were not required to study? Who would save them when it was time for college admissions and employment tests?

When I arrived in Florida, I expected those leaders and pastors to open their churches and organizations and operate after-school and Saturday academic centers, tutorial programs, and test-taking classes for the students. I wondered if the students believed they were better in sports than science, music than math, and rap than reading. I wondered if the students really felt that they'd given their best effort academically.

This chapter is examining the significance of causes. If the people involved feel that failure in test performance is caused by ineffective schools and teachers and inadequate funding, then the solutions have to address those causes.

If others think that the reason for poor performance is a lack of study time, then the solution has to be greater time on task.

A deeper issue is how much blame do we place on the perceived oppressor and how much do we place on ourselves? Human beings always want to exonerate themselves from responsibility and place the blame elsewhere. D'Souza asks: if racism disappeared tonight, would Black test scores improve and the number of Black companies increase? Would the Black family become stronger? Would Black on Black crime be reduced?

If racism ended tonight, would African Americans score better than 1200 on the SAT?

If there was no racism, would African Americans spend more than 4 percent of their $688 billion with each other?

If racism ended tonight, would it reduce the divorce rate from its present 66 percent?

If there was no racism, would Black on Black homicide be reduced from 1 out of every 21 African American males?

What do you think?

Two of the problems that I have with the conservatives is their lack of appreciation of history and their attempt to sound like nationalists, without providing programs and resources to correct the problems. Walter Williams says the major problem standing in the way of broader Black advancement will be solved only when Blacks finally recognize that our destinies lie in our own hands, and we alone can solve what are essentially Black problems—not Washington, politicians, or the intellectual elite.

That sounds like a Black nationalist. It sounds like Louis Farrakhan and the importance of doing for self. Where are Williams, Connerly, Steele, and D'Souza-led organizations dedicated to empowering the Black community? How many African Americans have they employed? How many students have they tutored? How many African American businesses have they created?

I have also been taught that if you want to assess someone's ideology, follow the money trail. The money trail will tell you who's funding the ideology. It reminds me of the classic parody of the Golden Rule: "Whoever has the gold, rules." I encourage all my readers to identify who's funding Walter Williams, Ward Connerly, Shelby Steele, Dinesh D'Souza, and others. None of them are funded by African American organizations.

The other concern I have about many leaders is their lack of appreciation of history. It sounds good to say, "If racism ended tonight, it would not correct the problems in the Black community." I too am concerned about brothers and sisters saying, "It's the Man, the White Man is holding me back." I often challenge those brothers and sisters and ask them, "What man are you talking about?" As psychiatrist Dr. Frances Welsing explains, if we call the White male "The Man," that eliminates us from being "The Man." We can then only be The Boy, but we can't be The Man.

From a Christian perspective, Joshua 1:5, says, "No man shall be able to stand before you, Joshua. As I was with Moses, I will also be with you." Verse 8 says, "This book of the law shall not depart from your mouth, but you shall meditate in it day and night and observe to do according to its will. And then you will make your way prosperous and then you will have good success." When Joshua 1:5 says "no man," that includes the White man. We give White people too much credit.

If Black people were inferior, there would be no reason to discriminate. The White baseball owners knew more about

Jackie Robinson than we did. They knew that Jackie Robinson—like Ben Carson and Mae Jamison—would do well. You don't discriminate against inferior people. Take that ridiculous statement that Blacks are lazy—if we were lazy, then why would Europeans travel three months on a slave ship named Jesus to bring back lazy people to work for them?

Obviously hindsight is 20/20, and I sincerely respect Thurgood Marshall, but he underestimated racism and White supremacy. Marshall naively thought that if Blacks simply were able to enter White schools, we would receive a quality education. Fifty years later, we realize that children can be attending an outwardly integrated school, but that school can be highly segregated internally because of tracking. You can have a school 50 percent White/50 percent Black in population, but within you can have a predominantly White-Asian advanced placement (AP), honors, and gifted and talented division; an integrated regular division; and a predominantly Black and Latino lower, remedial, and special education division.

In addition, Marshall underestimated racism and White supremacy in that you might be able to integrate schools, but it's more difficult to integrate neighborhoods. Andrew Hacker in the book *Two Nations*, along with numerous other authors, mentions a White threshold of 8 percent. When the African American population exceeds 8 percent, White flight begins.

Fifty years later, housing patterns are just as segregated, if not more so, than they were then. School funding is still based on housing patterns. Jonathan Kozol in the book *Savage Inequalities* documents that within the same state there are schools that allocate $15,000 to $20,000 per child while other school only allocate $3,000 to $6,000 per child. Some schools

# Causes

offer AP (advanced placement) programs in every class. In other schools, there are few if any AP classes available.

The NAACP won a lawsuit against the University of California at Berkeley. Numerous African American students who had earned a perfect 4.0 GPA (grade point average) in high school and scored 1200 or better on the SAT were denied admission to Ward Connerly's University of California-Berkeley. It turns out they were competing against students who almost had a 5.0 GPA due to higher numerical ratings for AP grades (e.g., 5 points are awarded for an AP "A" versus 4 points for a regular "A"). Now how can that be? How can a student master high school work, but not be admitted into the university? Because these young African Americans were competing against White youth who had taken AP classes, unavailable to most of the Black students, which made it possible for them to earn a 5.0 GPA.

Ward Connerly, the playing field is not level. These White students enjoyed 13 years (K-12) of affirmative action.

On the other hand, it does not mean that the White man is to blame for African Americans watching 38 hours of television, listening to 18 hours of rap music, and spending the rest of their time playing basketball, while only studying four hours per week. The White man did not make us watch television, listen to music, play basketball, and only study four hours a week. We give White people too much credit.

What Williams, Connerly, Steele, D'Souza, and others do not consider is the legacy of racism. Ending racism tonight does not eradicate its legacy. In a latter chapter entitled "Post-Traumatic Slavery Disorder/Africentricity," we will look at this in more detail.

The current problem started in 1865 when slavery ended, and its legacy continues. For 246 years in America, we had been taught the beauty and superiority of light skin, long straight hair, and blue eyes. We had been taught that Jesus Christ looked like Michelangelo's cousin and that our history began in 1619. That's part of the legacy of slavery.

We've been taught the Willie Lynch Syndrome, which looks for differences and does not operate in the spirit of unity. The conservatives like to compare immigrants to slaves. They love talking about immigrants who arrived in America and outperformed African Americans. Such immigrants even include Africans from the African continent. The media loves this argument because if liberals espouse that the major problem is racism, then how can Africans from Nigeria, Ghana, and Jamaica outperform, economically and educationally, African Americans? The fallacy of the argument is that you can't compare a small population that voluntarily comes here to a larger population that was forced to come. You can't compare a group that uses their culture to overcome racism in America with a group who's culture was stolen from them and in redress were given February, the shortest month of the year, to relearn their history.

As a scholar, I'm not afraid to read or debate anyone. I believe I can learn from anyone. While I disagree and feel it is unfair to compare immigrants to slaves, I believe that African Americans can utilize the immigrant model to overcome racism with the tools and mindset of culture. As a Christian, I'm always looking for good news, and that is good news. Racism can be defeated with the weapons of culture.

Asians outperform Whites on the SAT, regardless of their language barrier and the test being culturally biased against them. While African Americans associate being smart with being White, Asian adults teach their children to be the best. That is something that African Americans used to do, using

# Causes

Rule 110. Before Brown vs. Topeka, African American parents taught their children that the country is racist, and if you want to make it in America, you need to score more than 80, 90, or 100. You'd better be the best and score 110!

Asians believe in cooperative learning. It is very difficult to become an engineer or doctor studying alone. They also believe in time on task. Whatever you do most, you do best. Asians study far more than African Americans, Whites, and Hispanics. The tradition in Asian (and many other homes) is that parents are the primary educators of their children.

It's very disappointing to witness African American high school students taking the SAT in the second semester of their senior year for the first time. There are some children in America who take the PSAT (preliminary SAT) as early as fourth, fifth, or sixth grade. Research shows that the more times you take the test, the better your scores. Research also shows that when students take a college prep curriculum, i.e., three to four years of math or science, they score 100 points better on the SAT. Some African Americans think they're beating the system when they take fewer math and science courses. As Galatians 6:7 says, "God will not be mocked. You reap what you sow." If you only take one to three years of math or science, there's a very good chance that you won't score as high on the SAT or ACT.

I strongly encourage everyone to read the powerful book by Jimmy Dumas, *24 Reasons Why African Americans Suffer*. In the book he lists those reasons, which are as follows:

1. Lack of unity
2. Poor money management
3. Lack of education

4. Lack of discipline
5. Welfare
6. Teen pregnancy
7. Drugs
8. Lack of morals
9. The jinx of slavery
10. The crisis between African American men and women
11. The lack of spiritual vision
12. Confusion about the purpose of African American fraternities and sororities
13. Lack of investigative African American media
14. Lack of business resources
15. Insurance
16. Interracial marriage
17. Poor health
18. Loss of identity
19. Integration
20. Ignorance about African American contributions to science and technology
21. Lack of support from African American athletes
22. Desire for instant wealth
23. Homosexuality
24. Fear

Obviously, I cannot address these 24 reasons in the kind of detail Dumas does in his book. Throughout this book, we will look at some of these, and many we have addressed previously.

I said at the outset, that I almost wrote this book exclusively for the 20 percent of African Americans who live below the poverty line and the one million who earn less than $7,000 per

# Causes

year. In the book *The Truly Disadvantaged*, Julius Wilson offers the following quote:

> The culture of poverty is both an adaptation and a reaction of the poor to their marginal position and class stratified, highly individuated capitalistic society. The culture of poverty tends to perpetuate itself from generation to generation because of its effect on the children. By the time slum children are age six or seven, they have usually absorbed the basic values and attitudes of their subculture and are not psychologically geared to take full advantage of changing conditions or increased opportunities which may occur in their lifetime."[4]

Jesse Jackson, Jr., in many of his speeches loves talking about how success is predicated on the conjunction of opportunity with preparation. He emphasizes how important it is to be prepared. When opportunity knocks and preparation is present, success is near.

What can we do to alleviate the 20 percent of our race living below the poverty line? What's the agenda of Black leadership for this population? How do we address Julius Wilson's concern that by age six or seven basic values and attitudes have already been created? There are some neighborhoods where poverty is so concentrated that children observe adults who have never worked. Much more will be said about this in the "Family and Health" chapter. We'll also look at Oprah Winfrey's attempt to address the problem, as she realized that giving these families money to buy a house or a car was not enough and that classes on values needed to be provided.

As we conclude this chapter, let's return to Sizemore's paradigm, which we'll be using throughout this book.

# SOLUTIONS FOR BLACK AMERICA

| Problems | Causes | Solutions |
| --- | --- | --- |
| Education: 200 point differential on the SAT; 3 stanine difference on elementary school achievement tests | 1. Low income 2. Single parenting 3. Parental apathy 4. Lack of parental education 5. Inadequate school funding 6. Low teacher expectations 7. Time on task 8. Irrelevant Eurocentric Curriculum 9. Left-brained lesson plans 10. Negative peer pressure 11. Tracking | 1. Economic development; eradicate race discrimination 2. Premarital and marital counseling 3. Parent organizing and motivating 4. Greater access to GEDs, associate degrees, and scholarships 5. Abolish school funding based on property values and the state becomes the equalizer. 6. Teacher Expectation Student Achievement (TESA) 7. KIPP (Knowledge Is Power Program) 8. Africentricity 9. Whole-brained and right-brained lesson plans 10. Corporate learning 11. Abolish tracking |
| ✦✦✦✦✦✦✦✦✦ | ✦✦✦✦✦✦✦✦✦ | ✦✦✦✦✦✦✦✦ |
| Prison: 12% of the Black population; 50% of Black inmates are Black | 1. The 100:1 ratio of cocaine to crack 2. Mandatory minimum sentencing 3. Fatherlessness 4. Racial profiling 5. Inadequate legal defense 6. Little to no rehabilitation | 1. Raise crack to equal cocaine sentencing 2. Judge discretion 3. Village accountability 4. Fine racial profiling 5. Indiana model 6. Fund Rehabilitation |

# Causes

| Problems | Causes | Solutions |
|---|---|---|
| Poverty: 20% of African American adults; 50% of African American children<br><br>Unemployment: 12% of adults; 37% of teenagers Income Disparity: African Americans $32,000, White Americans $45,000 | 1. Racism 2. Miseducation 3. The feminization of poverty and fatherlessness 4. Teen pregnancy 5. Lack of values 6. Lack of transportation to suburbs 7. Lack of skills 8. Lack of entrepreneurship | 1. Greater resources and enforcement of EEOC 2. Enforce and adequately fund Leave No Child Behind programs. 3. Greater funding and enforcement of EEOC/Village Fathers/Project Alpha/Institute for Responsible Fathers 4. Goal setting/media campaign/A.C. Green's abstinence program 5. Africentricity 6. Expand business routes 7. Job training centers 8. NFTE (National Foundation for Teaching Entrepreneurship) |
| ✦✦✦✦✦✦✦✦✦✦ | ✦✦✦✦✦✦✦✦✦✦ | ✦✦✦✦✦✦✦✦✦ |
| Health: African Americans lead in 12 of 14 indicators, including heart disease, high blood pressure, kidney and liver disease, cancer, strokes, diabetes, and HIV.<br><br>HIV: African Americans represent 12% of the U.S. population. Black men comprise 43% of the cases; females, 64%. | 1. Obesity 2. Soul food diet 3. Lack of sexual protection 4. Inmates infected 5. Dirty needles | 1. Change diet, increase exercising 2. Less no pork, fried food, salt, and sugar 3. Greater media campaign and condom distribution 4. Better security; testing with results released to families 5. Medical treatment and clean needle program |

| Family: 66% divorce rate, 68% fatherlessness, 10% teen pregnancy | 1. Lack of pre-marital and marital counseling 2. Selfishness 3. Lack of goals/poor self-esteem | 1. Pre-marital counseling before date can be secured 2. Salvation 3. goal setting/ Africentricity |

Before we look at solutions in full detail in the remaining chapters, there is one other issue that deserves a closer look. The next chapter examines integration and its impact on the Black community.

# CHAPTER 3

# INTEGRATION REVISITED

My late aunt, Lucille Johnston, and my uncle, Bill Johnston, were born in the early 1900s in the eastern part of Texas. They were taught by some of the best teachers America has ever experienced. They were nurtured, encouraged, and given high expectations. They were taught Rule 110. Back in the Jim Crow era, African American children were taught that being Black meant being the best. They were reminded that if they were inferior, then why are Whites discriminating against them?

Before Brown vs. Topeka, teachers encouraged and taught African American students that you don't measure a school based on facilities. You measure a school based on teacher expectations and student performance. Teachers would tell Aunt Lu and Uncle Bill, "We may have a one-room school shack and have to use White leftover school books, but it does not mean that I can't teach and you can't learn."

Rule 110 meant just that. Seventy, 80, and 90 were unacceptable. The objective was to score over 100. Students were encouraged to seek projects for extra credit to surpass 100. In the early 1920s throughout Black America, because of segregation, African Americans with PhDs lived on the same block as those with no degrees and, like their less-educated neighbors, could not find work. DuBois' Talented Tenth and Jesus' least of these lived on the same block. Many African American youth whose parents were not doing well financially had positive African American role models who lived on their block.

After Aunt Lu and Uncle Bill graduated from high school with honors, the University of Texas was unavailable to them. Their choices were limited in Texas to Texas Southern and Prairie View University. They both chose Prairie View, and again they performed with honors.

During their college experience, not only were they limited as to where they could attend, but also as to the major they could pursue. During the Jim Crow era, African Americans seldom majored in business, engineering, accounting, finance, marketing, etc., because Wall Street and the Fortune 500 were off limits. Most African Americans majored in education, nursing, and religion. A few of them pursued law and medicine. Those that pursued those majors knew they would be restricted to the African American community.

The bulk of African American college students during the Jim Crow, Plessy vs. Ferguson era, majored in education. Ironically, the African American community benefited from this dynamic. The best Black minds in the country were in the classroom. Aunt Lu and Uncle Bill benefited from their teachers. And when they became teachers—both taught in Huntsville, Texas, and married there—literally every African American child in Huntsville benefited from these two brilliant minds who had had vocational limitations placed on them. They had a tremendous impact on African American children.

It is now 2004. Bill and Lucille Johnston's granddaughter is a graduating senior in Huntsville, Texas. Things have drastically changed. There has been a 66 percent decline in African American teachers since 1954. Their granddaughter has experienced very few African American teachers. Because of her strong family background, her parents have tried their best to supplement her educational experience. The school system wanted to keep her in regular classes, but her mother literally demanded that she receive the opportunity to be placed in gifted and talented classes.

After integration, schools appeared integrated on the outside—50 percent White, 50 percent Black—but on the inside, it was predominantly Whites in advanced placement, honors, and gifted and talented classes and predominantly African Americans in lower, remedial, and special education classes. The challenge for the Johnston's granddaughter was that she had been in gifted and talented, honors, and advanced placement classes with very few of her African American peers. Her parents tried to supplement her education with programs like Jack and Jill and church activities. It was also a challenge because she lived in a very affluent suburb of Huntsville where there's only one other African American neighbor on the block.

With their granddaughter, there are no African American males in her gifted and talented, honors, and advanced placement classes. There are few teachers like Bill Johnston available, and boys have had a difficult time matriculating through this new school system. Bill Johnston had numerous African American male teachers, but today most boys seldom experience an African American male teacher. Many of the boys live in the ghetto of Huntsville, Texas, in housing developments. Housing developments in the North are vertical, while in the South they're horizontal. The concentration of poverty goes deep.

The Black boy observes very few African American men in the neighborhood. The few available are unemployed. It's been a challenge for males to graduate from high school. Many boys are retained in elementary school, placed in special education classes, and doped with Ritalin. Many males believe their only options are the NBA, a rap contract, drugs, UPS, the military, or McDonalds.

The Johnston's granddaughter is considering Harvard or Spelman. She wants to become an investment broker on Wall Street. She wants to pursue an MBA. She's leaning toward Harvard because she feels it has more to offer and will provide a better networking experience into Wall Street. Often she wonders why she is one of the few African Americans in AP classes, and she doesn't know who she will go to the prom with because the pickings are very slim. That may be one reason why she hasn't given up on considering Spelman, which would give her an opportunity to be with the men of Morehouse.

I wish the late Thurgood Marshall, the brilliant lawyer and Supreme Court Justice, were alive to witness what has happened in the past 50 years. Hindsight is always 20/20. Thurgood Marshall naively thought that in winning Brown vs. Topeka, equality would be achieved simply by allowing African Americans to attend the same schools as Whites. Let us consider Webster's definition of integrate: "To remove the legal and social barriers imposing segregation upon racial groups so as to permit free and equal association, to abolish segregation from school, neighborhood, etc." Integration: "The bringing of different racial and ethnic groups into free and equal association."

We have never had integration in America. Where do we place the blame? On ignorance. If Blacks had known the truth, we would have sued for facilities instead of integration. When Thurgood Marshall was alive and pursuing Brown vs. Topeka, there were a large number of African American teachers, equivalent to, if not greater, than the number of African American students. I wonder how Thurgood Marshall would feel if he were alive and I told him that African American students now comprise 17 percent of the national student population, but African American teachers are only 6 percent of the teaching population and African American male teachers only 1 percent. Furthermore, there has been a 66 percent decline in African American teachers since the infamous 1954 Brown vs. Topeka decision. The future of the Black race, specifically African American boys, lies in the hands of White female teachers. This was the major catalyst for my previous book, *Black Students—Middle-Class Teachers*. The first encounter many White teachers have with African American children is in the classroom. They do not live in the African American community, and they have not taken any classes in African American studies. Yet they now have the right to label children ADD (attention deficit disorder), ADHD (attention deficit hyperactive disorder), LD (learning disorder), and BD (behavior disorder) and suspend and expel students.

There has not only been a decline in the quantity of African American teachers, but also a decline in teaching quality. We have fewer Lucille and Bill Johnstons teaching African American students. These were stellar teachers who literally in college and graduate school kept a 4.0 GPA. Today, many African Americans choose education because they feel the curriculum is less rigorous. They enjoy the short work hours and the three months of vacation. There have been numerous research documents that illustrate that the GPA of teachers is lower than the GPA of those in engineering, accounting, business, computers, medicine, and law.

I wonder how Thurgood Marshall would feel if he were alive and discovered that not only do we have less African American minds in the classroom, but that the quality of teaching has declined. Before 1954, there was very little tracking (students are divided based on perceived abilities and test scores) in schools. After 1954, tracking has increased tremendously. We have not achieved integration if schools are highly segregated on the inside, based on tracking.

I wonder how Thurgood Marshall would feel if he walked into an integrated high school and observed the racial make-up of students in advanced placement, honors, and gifted and talented and compared that to the racial make-up of students in remedial, lower track, and special education classes. Can you imagine Thurgood Marshall sitting down with some Black students in regular and remedial classes only to hear them say that the Johnston's granddaughter is "acting White" because she's in gifted and talented, honors, and advanced placement classes?

Ironically, one of the pieces of evidence used in Brown vs. Topeka was Kenneth Clark's doll theory. The low self-esteem of African American children was illustrated by their choice of dolls that did not look like them. From a psychological perspective, you wonder where the rationale for overcoming this problem will come from. Is the assumption that attending integrated schools will reduce the chances of African American children choosing White dolls?

Fifty years after Brown vs. Topeka, African American children are now associating being smart with acting White. They now believe that speaking standard English is speaking White. When African American students have aspirations beyond sports and social clubs and choose to participate in science fairs, debate teams, and academic clubs, they are accused by peers of acting White. Was this the objective of integration?

If we look at the doll theory and dialectical terms like "good hair" and "pretty eyes," I wonder how Kenneth Clark and Thurgood Marshall would feel if they saw videos on BET, MTV, and VH-1, where seldom if ever do you see an African

# Integration Revisited

American female darker than the male. I believe that African Americans will not be free until they believe that Whoopi Goldberg looks as good as Halle Berry. In a later chapter on Africentricity, we will look at this and other dynamics in greater detail.

Another expression of tracking has been the creation of magnet schools. If dividing a school based on ability is not enough, then giving those in the highest ability grouping the most experienced teachers and giving those in the lowest ability grouping the least experienced teachers puts the nail in the coffin. In my hometown of Chicago, there are approximately 60 high schools. Ninety percent of those schools are inferior, unsuccessful, and inadequate. The remaining 10 percent are primarily magnet schools. In Chicago 85 to 90 percent of the students are of color. Only 10 percent of the students are White. Therefore, most students of color are limited in their ability to attend the magnet schools because of the need to make the schools racially balanced. As a result, magnet schools seek out White students and limit Black students. In addition, for some strange reason, in a school district 90 percent of color, the teaching staff cannot exceed 60 percent African American. As a result, schools and principals are forced to do whatever they can to increase the percentage of White teachers in their schools. Thurgood Marshall had no idea that Brown vs. Topeka would create these kinds of challenges.

You can't legislate racism. Previously, I mentioned Hacker, who indicated that the White threshold for integration hovers near 8 percent. Whenever a neighborhood exceeds 8 percent African American population, White flight begins. Thurgood Marshall did not consider the impact of housing patterns on school districts. You can't integrate a school if integration does not exist in the neighborhood. Since 1954, housing patterns have become more segregated. As I mentioned earlier, African Americans should have sued for facilities instead of integration.

In Jonathan Kozol's book *Savage Inequalities* and in my book *Black Students—Middle-Class Teachers*, we document the tremendous funding disparity in schools based on housing patterns. You have two schools in the state. One school is in an affluent suburb and allocates $15,000 to $20,000 per child. Another school is in the inner city in the same state and allocates $3,000 to $6,000 per child. This is a clear illustration of Plessy vs. Ferguson: separate and unequal. Brown vs. Topeka does not address this issue because you can't force people to live in a particular neighborhood. Schools presently are funded based on property taxes, and states have not provided the equalizer.

In addition, many Whites created private schools in order to remain in their neighborhood without their children having to attend an integrated school. Some people are fearful that vouchers are another way that Whites could use public monies to attend private schools. I believe that Cleveland, Milwaukee, and Washington have illustrated that if legislation is written in such a way that only those parents who live near or below the poverty line are eligible for vouchers, we can circumvent that problem.

I also wish that I could share with Thurgood Marshall the impact that integration has had on Black colleges. Before 1965, 90 percent of African American college students attended a Black college. This explains why Lucille and Bill Johnston both attended Prairie View University. In 2004, only 16 percent of African American college students attend a Black college. There has been a tremendous decline in the percentage of

# Integration Revisited

African American students attending Black colleges in spite of the fact that they produce 30 percent of the graduates.

In addition, Black colleges produce 75 percent of the African Americans who pursue graduate studies. I wish I could give Thurgood Marshall a tour of Bloomfield State, Tennessee State, and Kentucky State, just to name a few. In 1954, Bloomfield State had a 100 percent African American population. In 1967, it had dropped to 38 percent. In 1978, it was 14 percent. Presently, only 7 percent of this historical Black college's population is African American—and they have no African American faculty members. Nationwide, 18 percent of the students at historically Black colleges are White, and 13 percent are foreign born.[5]

Not only has there been a tremendous decline in the African American student population, there has also been a decline in African American faculty. In 1954, more than 90 percent of the faculty was African American. Presently, that figure is only 46 percent. Many of the historically Black colleges are facing severe financial crises. Some of them have closed since 1954. Some have merged with other schools. Fifteen percent are on probation. Many of my friends who are Black college presidents have told me that they spend more time raising money than providing educational leadership.

I wish that Thurgood Marshall could attend a meeting of the Minority Student Achievement Network (MSAN). This organization operates primarily in affluent suburbs. They believe in integration. They believed in Thurgood Marshall. They believe in the American Dream. They thought that if their children attended a school in an affluent town or suburb—Evanston, Illinois; Cambridge, Massachusetts; Ann Arbor, Michigan; Berkeley, California; Shaker Heights or Cleveland Heights, Ohio; and similar other—their problems would be solved. The reality is that even when living in the same affluent community and attending the same school, there is a racial disparity in academic performance. The late John Ogbu wrote the book *Black American Students in an Affluent Suburb*. He documented that the achievement gap widens with greater income. He was brought in as a consultant in Shaker Heights to explain this disparity. Ogbu felt that the most significant factors were lack of African American parental involvement and negative peer pressure. While I agree with the above, I believe more significant factors were tracking, lower expectations based on race, inadequate amount of time on task for instruction, an irrelevant Eurocentric curriculum, and an incongruence between teacher pedagogy and student learning styles.

In this chapter on integration, not only do we need to look at it from an educational perspective, but also from an economic one. I challenge any African American in 2004 to provide a Black business district as viable as the Black Wall Street in Tulsa, Oklahoma, in 1904. The same applies for the Hayti District in Durham, Beale Street in Memphis, and Auburn Avenue in Atlanta.

In 1904, Black Wall Street in Tulsa only had 11,000 African Americans. Long before the Montgomery bus boycott of 1955, African Americans in Tulsa owned their own bus line, hospital, two newspapers, two theaters, three drug stores, four hotels, 150 buildings, and large numbers of offices that housed doctors, lawyers, and other businesses. Black money was spent among Black people. Today, it has been said that you'd have to return to Jim Crow to increase the percentage of money that African Americans spend with each other. We will earn more money in 2004 than we did in 1904, but now we will only spend about 4 percent of that money with African

# Integration Revisited

American businesses. I wish Thurgood Marshall could see the tremendous dichotomy between Benton Harbor, Michigan, and its next door neighbor, St. Joseph; Gary, Indiana, and Merrillville; East Palo Alto, California, and Palo Alto.

The same is applicable to the Negro Baseball League. Before 1947, when Jackie Robinson entered major league baseball, there were 4,000 African American players. There were 20 teams, which means 20 Black owners. There were vendors who made large amounts of money at the games. Many of the teams owned their own stadiums. The Negro Baseball League won 60 percent of the games that it played against the White leagues. As I said earlier, if we were inferior, there would be no need for discrimination. They knew Jackie Robinson, Josh Gibson, and Satchel Paige were not inferior.

Things have changed since Satchel Paige pitched in the Negro Baseball League. Kobe Bryant bought his wife Vanessa a $4 million ring as partial payment for his adulterous act. By the way, $4 million could take 571 families off welfare and live above the poverty line.

A lot has happened since 1954. Lucille Johnston attended a one-room school shack in Huntsville, Texas. Her grand-daughter attends an affluent high school and lives on a block containing only one other African American family. There are no African American businesses in her suburb. Even if she wanted to and had the commitment to support African American businesses, there would be none to support. The only way for her to support African American businesses would be to travel into the ghettos of the Black community.

I wish Martin Luther King could walk down all the streets named after him. I think he would break down and cry. Many of the buildings are abandoned and boarded up. The businesses are primarily liquor stores, barbershops, beauty shops, greasy

43

fried-food joints, and funeral homes. In the earlier "Problems" and "Causes" chapters, we mentioned that 32 percent of the African American community is living very well and is making in excess of $50,000 per year. Many of them live in communities where there are few to no African American businesses.

In contrast, 20 percent of African Americans, including 50 percent of our children, live below the poverty line. They live in those communities where there are few remaining African American businesses. The variety of services and products is less than adequate. In a latter chapter on "Economics," we will look at this in much more detail.

Let me return to a poignant question. Is it true that African Americans would have to return to Jim Crow in order to increase the 3 percent that we now spend with each other? Did we make the right decision to abandon the Negro Baseball League so that Jackie Robinson and a few individuals could pursue their careers in sports to the demise of the Black baseball owners, vendors, and suppliers? If you ask Bonds or Sheffield and numerous others with multi-million-dollar contracts, there is no need for discussion. There is no way that the Negro Baseball League was going to pay Jackie Robinson what the Brooklyn Dodgers paid him. Major league stadiums are larger, ticket prices are greater, and they have cash cows like television contracts.

The decision to integrate has been beneficial for a few. From a collective standpoint, we have to ask ourselves, how many jobs will Bonds, Sheffield, and other stars create in comparison to how many people would be employed if we had maintained the Negro Baseball League? The same alternatives might be considered for the NFL or the NBA. I also wonder if the NBA could survive if 84 percent of its

# Integration Revisited

players, which just happen to be African American, would no longer play? The same applies to the NFL, where African Americans constitute 67 percent of the players.

While Brown vs. Topeka was a very critical, historical moment in the African American experience, I also believe that Montgomery, December 1, 1955, was also significant. For 381 days, we shut Montgomery down. Rosa Parks had made a decision, the same decision that several of her peers had made in earlier years, but this time there was tremendous follow-up and the leadership was stronger. For 381 days, we did not ride their buses. We created alternative transportation. The Montgomery power brokers came to their senses and realized it was better for African Americans to sit wherever they wanted than for them to lose money.

The critical question that African Americans need to ask themselves is how concerned are we about where we sit versus what we own? We now have the right to sit wherever we want. We have the right to sit on the first floor of any theater in America. We have the right to sit at any restaurant, even though there have been some challenges concerning service.

One of the things I respect most about the Jewish community is that they study their history. It has always been amazing to me that most Americans know that six million Jews died in Germany, but do not know how many Africans died in America during the slave trade. The Jews' motto is "Never forget. If we forget Germany we lose Israel."

Why don't we want to watch "Eyes on the Prize," "Roots," "Mississippi Burning," and similar movies so that we can understand our story? We have a similar motto. We just drop the word "never" because we want to forget. When I talk to African American elders, they say they can't watch those stories or read their history because it makes them mad. The Jews don't get mad; they get smart. A people who do not know their history are destined to make the same mistakes over and over and over again.

Did we make the right decision with Brown vs. Topeka? Did we make the right decision in Montgomery, Alabama?

In my hometown, Chicago, Mayor Harold Washington had died. The city constitution required that the City Council of 50 members would decide who would be the next mayor. There were enough African Americans there to select the next mayor, but many of them disagreed with each other. There was a split, and the larger White community saw it. They knew that the next time there was an election, they could win. Jesse Jackson, Sr., kept telling the Black City Council members, "We have the keys. We can discuss the disagreement between the two African American candidates later. Let's go home tonight. We have the keys."

The lesson we did not learn that night was the lesson of operational unity. African Americans need to understand that we may be discussing ten issues and may disagree on nine, but let's work on the issue we agree on in a spirit of operational unity. There is no need to play the game of who's Blacker than whom. I've been to conferences where, in spite of all the major problems going on in the African American community, the issue that divided the group was whether Africentricity was going to be spelled Afro or Afri.

Did we make the right decision to send Jackie Robinson into major league baseball, or should we have maintained the Negro Baseball League? On one level this could be a rhetorical question because if the stars wanted to be in the major leagues, then the Negro Baseball League couldn't have been maintained.

Here's the million-dollar question that I want to ask Black America: What is your definition of freedom? Is it going to White schools? Living in White neighborhoods? Buying from White stores? Sitting on White buses? Dining in White restaurants? Vacationing in White hotels? What is your definition of freedom?

In the book *Black Labor, White Wealth,* Claud Anderson says the following:

> The Black civil rights movement, though spectacularly successful in many respects, had at least four flaws that diminished the accomplishments of the movement and left critical imperatives in Black America. The movement's Black leadership focused its entire weight of resources on achieving integration. They believed, perhaps naively, that by removing all the symbols of Jim Crowism and acquiring access to various segments of White society, Black people would gain equality. Black leaders failed to focus on neutralizing the forces behind Jim Crowism or developing effective strategies for Black America to use in dealing with the problems that spring forth from the maldistribution and racist control of wealth, power, and resources in America. They failed to develop a long-term national plan with goals and strategies spelling out where Blacks ought to be going and how best to get there. In addition, Black leaders failed to construct a national network of institutions to train new generations of Blacks who could successfully assume leadership positions and implement a national plan for Black empowerment.[6]

Stokely Carmichael in the powerful book, *Ready For Revolution*, says,

> According to the advocates of integration, social justice will be accomplished by "integrating the Negro into the mainstream institutions of the society from which he has been traditionally excluded." It is very significant that each time I have heard this formulation, it has been in terms of "the Negro," the individual Negro, rather than in terms of

the community. This concept of integration had to be based on the assumption that there was nothing of value in the Negro community and that little of value could be created among Negroes, so the thing to do was to siphon off the "acceptable" Negroes into the surrounding middle-class White community. Thus the goal of the movement for integration was simply to loosen up the restrictions barring the entry of certain Negroes into the White community . . . only a small select group of Negroes. Its goal was to make the White community accessible to "qualified" Negroes, and presumably each year a few more Negroes armed with their passports—a couple of university degrees—would escape into middle-class America and adopt the attitudes and life styles of that group; and one day the Harlems and the Wattses would stand empty, a tribute to the success of integration. This is simply neither realistic nor particularly desirable. You can integrate communities, but you assimilate individuals.[7]

## Oba T'Shaka reinforces this point with the following:

Youth who made up the rank and file as well as the leadership of the civil rights movement entered the movement thinking that their adult leadership had correctly thought out the direction of the civil rights movement. Later these youth discovered that the civil rights model was deficient. For the civil rights leadership, the ultimate political goal was integration and equality in every phase of life. This meant that Black communities and Black institutions were temporary places that would eventually be torn down when the era of integration arrived. This outlook led to the conclusion that group power, economically and politically, was unimportant. National civil rights leadership offered no direction for building cooperative economic power. And when the dissenting member of this group, DuBois, did put forth an economic development model, he was kicked out of the NAACP.[8]

48

# Integration Revisited

That is a profound analysis. The ultimate objective of integration is to eliminate Black communities and Black institutions. If the objective of integration was to allow the Johnston's granddaughter to attend Harvard, then there's no need for Spelman. As a result, we now see the tremendous decline in the number of Black colleges, Black students, and Black faculty.

In the state of Mississippi, we won the court case. There's been tremendous discrimination and lack of funding for the three Black colleges in the state. If our objective is integration, in the spirit of Rodney King ("Can't we all just get along?"), then those three Black colleges should now be authorized, charged, and required to increase the percentage of White students attending—and that includes scholarships.

Amos Wilson provides further clarity on this issue:

> Black leadership is typified by the NAACP, the Urban League, Operation PUSH, and others who not only neither advocate nor aggressively promulgate an economic program for the African American community, but actively fight against such a program. They seem to perceive the problems facing the Black community as essentially problems having to do with civil rights, human rights, and moral turpitude, i.e., the failure of America to live out up to its highly publicized moral, constitutional, political, and civic values...the programs these leaders have imposed on the African American community [constitute what] political scientists have aptly captioned "noneconomic liberalism." The emphasis on noneconomic liberalism as the guiding philosophy of responsible Black bourgeois leadership involves the projecting of strong reformist impulses in the realms of civil liberties, race relations, and foreign affairs but not in the basic distribution of wealth and power. The assimilationist, integrationist, Black bourgeois leadership would essentially reduce all the racial economic subordination and exploitation of African

Americans to race discrimination in employment, public and private accommodations, [and] vehemently oppose the self-help economic ideologies of Booker T. Washington, Marcus Garvey, and those [who] preceded and followed them, popularly known as Black nationalists. Moralistic coloring of this leadership establishment follows from its belief that separation by race is morally reprehensible, that ethnic exclusivity is morally unconscionable. More pertinent, however, is its belief that racism, especially in the form of White supremacy and all that it implies, represents a fundamentally moral problem, a problem founded on racial prejudice, stereotypes, deviations from Christian ethics, lack of racial or humanistic enlightenment. The assimilationist moralistic establishment essentially overlooks the economic rationale for one race dominating another.[9]

I'm invited to speak at numerous conferences, seminars, and symposiums on multi-culturalism, diversity, inclusion, and race relations. In 90 percent of my presentations I try to be informative, enlightening, and entertaining. In closing, I challenge the audience and share with them the imperative that now that we've had this great intellectual exercise and masturbation on race relations, it's time to get to the heart of the issue. The issue is power, not racism. Slavery was driven by economics and power. When Harold Washington was the mayor of Chicago, there were 50 wards in the city, 34 of color and 16 White. There was a $3 billion budget, but for some strange reason the 16 White wards had control of $2 billion of it.

# Integration Revisited

Harold Washington, in the spirit of Ma'at (African value system), simply said, "When I become mayor each ward will receive one-fiftieth of the $3 billion budget." Well, that seemed fair to people who were naïve and did not understand power. The people who did, realized that they were going to lose $1 billion. They gave Harold Washington the blues and fought him every step of the way.

Often schools will bring me in to discuss how we can improve the academic achievement of the children, but they do not want to address the need to increase the number of African American faculty. Because then we're talking about power and employment.

In 1896 with Plessy vs. Ferguson, in 1954 with Brown vs. Topeka, and in 1955 with the Montgomery bus boycott, the objective was clear and the enemy could be easily defined. Very similar to South Africa and apartheid, it was easy to recognize the enemy. Before 1865 and the end of slavery, it was also easy to recognize the enemy. They were the chains on our wrists and ankles.

Who is the enemy in 2004? What are the challenges?

If a Black woman in 1804 Mississippi was walking through the fields late at night by herself and someone was walking toward her, she would have wished to see a Black man first, a Black woman second, a White woman third, and the last person she would have wanted to see in a Mississippi cotton field in 1804 would have been a White male. If you asked her that same question today, but changed the locale to Beale Street in Memphis, Auburn in Atlanta, State Street in Chicago, or Martin Luther King Street all over America, she would say send the Black female first, the White female second, the White male third, and the last person she'd want to see late at night by herself on Martin Luther King Avenue would be the Black male.

Much has happened between 1804 and 2004. If a Black candidate is running for mayor of a major city that has never experienced a Black in that office, it's almost like a revolution has come to town. Many African Americans will come out to vote for the very first time. They naively believe that when a Black mayor is elected, housing projects will come tumbling down like Jericho, they will live in better conditions, be gainfully employed, and power will be equally distributed. Sadly, they find out that when Black mayors are elected, very little changes, especially for the "least of these."

Granted, the Talented Tenth secures more contracts, but for the masses of African Americans, especially the 20 percent who live below the poverty line with 50 percent of all African American children, very little changes. In many cities, African Americans are now mayors and superintendents of police, fire, and education. Yet, very little has changed for the masses. In later chapters we will look at the dichotomy between economics and political power. Suffice it to say that it is difficult for African Americans to wail, "The Man is holding me back," when The Man may look like us. What man are we talking about, anyway, if Blacks are mayors, superintendents, and principals? We are The Man that the sister is afraid to see at 10:00 at night. In many low-income communities in Black America, the only non-African Americans they see are the Arab and Asian business owners. In some neighborhoods, they don't see Whites at all.

To further complicate this matter, we have people like Ward Connerly, who not only is against affirmative action, but also supports Proposition 54, designed to eliminate race as a factor

# Integration Revisited

in classifying populations as well as their income levels, education, and other significant factors of life. It was very disappointing that Ward Connerly, along with the media, was not honest on the University of Michigan affirmative action case. For some strange reason, the media emphasized that applicants received 20 points extra in the admission process based on race. You also received 20 points if you were poor, 20 points if you were an athlete, and 16 points based on where you lived in the state and if your parents were alumni. The media loves using people like Ward Connerly, Shelby Steele, Walter Williams, and others to espouse their positions because it makes it difficult for the larger Black community to determine the enemy.

In the next chapter on "Education" and all following chapters we will look only at solutions. Sizemore said, "Solutions are only successful if we agree on what caused the problems." In these initial chapters I have tried to create an environment for understanding the problems and their causes, although I'm not naive enough to think that we're now all in agreement on those factors.

I believe the major cause for 1 percent of the population owning 48 percent of the wealth, and 10 percent owning 86 percent of the wealth, and the widening schism between the Black haves and the Black have nots, is power. The educational disparity in America is a result of power. The same demon that drives racism drives sexism and classism. Ephesians 6:12 says, "We struggle not against flesh and blood, but against principalities and rulers in high places." It concerns me that African American males can see racism among Whites, but cannot see sexism in the Black church, community organizations, and in their homes.

People who love freedom not only want it for themselves, but they want it for everyone. It disappoints me that many Black leaders want school choice for their biological children, but do not want choice for low-income children.

# CHAPTER 4

# DUCATION

Let me quickly share the education problems so that the remaining part of this chapter can be reserved exclusively for solutions.

1.  63 percent of African American fourth-grade students are below grade level in reading.
2.  61 percent of eighth-grade African American students are below grade level in math.
3.  SAT averages: Asians 1083; Whites 1063; Hispanics 903; African Americans 857.
4.  Only 56 percent of African Americans graduate from high school at the age of 18.
5.  27 percent of African Americans earn their G.E.D. by the age of 25.
6.  Only 21 percent of African American high school graduates are able to take college level courses.
7.  African American students comprise 17 percent of the students in public schools, but 32 percent of the Black students are suspended, 41 percent are placed in special education, and only 3 percent are engaged in gifted and talented programs.
8.  Only 6 percent of America's teachers are African American. Only 1 percent are African American males.
9.  The future of the Black race lies in the hands of the 83 percent of elementary school teachers who are White and female.[10]

A Jewish mother is walking down the street with her two young sons. A passerby asks her how old are the boys. "The doctor is three," says the mother. "The lawyer is two." I am reminded of Proverbs 18:21: "Death and life are in the power of the tongue." Hebrews 11:2 says: "God framed the world by His words."

Satan will try to convince us that sticks and stones may break your bones, but words will never hurt you. I believe that is a lie from the pit of hell. Words are powerful. Words create images, visions, and goals. You, the reader, can remember things that were said about you, positively or negatively, decades ago. It hurts me when I hear African American parents make derogatory comments about their children.

As a national consultant to schools, I am very critical of what they are not doing for African American children in grades K-12. However, schools cannot be faulted and held responsible for what parents are not doing between infancy and five years old. There are studies on Head Start and Cradle to the Classroom that document that some children enter kindergarten having heard 500,000 more words than their classmates. These children were blessed with parents who spoke that many more words than other parents. We won't even begin to discuss the tone and nature of those words. The Jewish mother is sowing into her children's lives the positive notion that they will become doctors and lawyers. On the other hand, some parents are making derogatory comments such as, "You'll never be nothing, you're just like your daddy."

Beyond the 500,000 extra words heard, some children enter kindergarten with up to 20,000 hours of literacy. They had a book in their hands early on and their parents read to them. Unfortunately, other children enter kindergarten with less than two hours of literacy. It's very important for African

# Education

Americans reading this book to realize the importance of speaking positive words to their children and exposing their children to literature at a very early age.

There has been excellent research coming from Cradle to the Classroom, Jet Set, and First Steps (early intervention programs for infants through age three) showing that their students have a much higher graduation rate than their peers and less repeat teen pregnancies. Their children are performing better in school. The research becomes cloudier as it relates to Head Start. From its beginning in 1965, more than 20 million at-risk children and their families have been impacted by Head Start. Some of the critics of Head Start have said that the educational benefits have been marginal. In defense of the program, Head Start is more than an educational program. It is also designed to empower parents and to teach them to be more active in their child's academic development. As many as 1.3 million single mothers of Head Start children have become volunteers in the program. In addition, many of them have become Head Start teacher assistants, teachers, and directors.

A study was conducted in Ypsilanti, Michigan, that monitored Head Start children over an 18-year period. This population had a much lower drop-out rate than those who did not have the privilege of attending Head Start. Unfortunately, many African American children do not receive proper medical treatment in the early years, and Head Start has also created an opportunity for those medical services to be provided.

An educational criticism of Head Start is that certain research findings have shown that some Head Start children are only at the 23rd percentile when entering kindergarten and are not capable of handling academic kindergarten work.

Another study done by John Meier found that kindergarteners who completed Head Start scored 9 percent higher in literacy and language skills than other low-income students and 7 percent higher in number recognition and counting.

I mentioned health-related concerns earlier. In 2003, more than 800,000 poor children received medical and dental screenings and immunizations; 65,000 received mental health assessments; 75,000 received assistance with speech or language impairments. I believe Head Start needs to be maintained and should not be controlled by states, which would dilute the program. It is amazing how we can become so critical of Head Start when there is no comparison between the efficacy of Head Start and prison. Where is the outcry and backlash against an 85 percent prison recidivism rate while spending $28,000 per inmate? In contrast, we spend less than $7,000 per child in Head Start.

Many parents have internalized their importance as the primary educators of their children. They have decided that they are not going to give their children to a school district if they feel it is not in the child's best interest. In my book *Black Students—Middle-Class Teachers* I said that encountering two consecutive years of ineffective teachers could destroy a child for life. (I wonder how many parents are aware that their child might be in a classroom with an ineffective teacher?) With this risk in mind, many parents have decided that their children's future is too important to leave their youngsters in an academic setting that is not conducive to their children's learning. As a result, it is estimated that more than 100,000 African American children, and 2 million children nationwide, are being home-schooled. There are numerous Black home-school networks that can be contacted online.

# Education

In the excellent book Morning by *Morning We Home Schooled Our Sons to Ivy League Schools* by Paula Penn-Nabrit, she indicates the following lessons learned:

1. Use time wisely.
2. Education is more than academics.
3. The idea of "parent as teacher" doesn't have to end at kindergarten.
4. The family is our introduction to the community.
5. Extended family is a safety net.
6. Children do better in environments designed for them.
7. Travel is an education.
8. Athletics is more than competitive sports.
9. The secret to SATs and ACTs is test early and often.[11]

One of the major insights that home-school parents have realized is that they do not have to be the teacher in every subject. While it's easier to be the teacher when children are in primary and intermediate grades, for many parents it is very challenging in the advanced grades. In reviewing home-school literature, we find that many parents have become CEOs and managers of the home-school process. They utilize museums and local colleges and hire tutors to teach subjects in which they feel inadequate. Many home-school children will be tutored in math by a college student and the librarian will present storytelling hours, while a music school will be enlisted for piano, the YMCA for martial arts and gym, the planetarium or aquarium for science, and the Internet and purchased software packages for myriad subjects. Many parents, depending on their work schedules and the children's ages and maturation, will leave the assignments up to their children, while they coordinate the schedules of the various outside professionals.

Many assume that parents who home-school consist of a husband who is the sole provider and a mother who has a college degree and is able to stay home and educate the children from birth to high-school graduation. That would be the ideal scenario. The opposite is a working-class single mother who holds down a traditional 9 to 5 job, but has found creative ways to home-school her son who the school felt was hyperactive and a candidate for special education and Ritalin. We need more media stories describing how a young, low-income, single female parent home-schooled her son to a college scholarship. What did this single mother do?

While individual stories can vary, let me give you the typical scenario. Mom takes her nine-year-old son to her mother's house on the way to work. She has bought textbooks and workbooks and has borrowed library books for him. She has installed a computer at her home and at her mother's house, or has chosen to use a laptop. Throughout the day, she is in communication with her son. Very similar to a class schedule, she has designed the program so that from 9:00 to 11:00 her son will be reading a book and writing a report. At 11:00 he is supposed to call her (or vice versa) to briefly review what he has learned from that assignment. Then he can take a brief break to interact with his grandmother. Between 11:15 and 11:30 he moves on to his math assignment. One to two hours later he calls his mother back to share what he has learned in math. He then has lunch with his grandmother. At approximately 2:00 he turns on his computer and goes to the sites that his mother has designated or uses the various software packages that have been provided.

# Education

At 4:00 his grandmother takes him to the YMCA, where they have arts and crafts, martial arts, and basketball. His mother picks him up from the YMCA at 6:00 and takes him home. Saturday is designated science day, and she takes him to a museum, aquarium, planetarium, and/or the zoo. It's also her opportunity over the weekend, along with some evenings, to review all of his work and to prepare lesson plans for the following week. She has also acquired standardized tests online. On a monthly basis, she tests her student and is proud to report that her fourth-grade son who the school recommended for special education is on a sixth-grade level in reading and a seventh-grade level in math.

During the summer, unlike public schools that close for 12 weeks because they're still based on the agrarian economy, she maintains this schedule. Her son is able to play in the park in mid-afternoon. She only has two weeks of vacation, and she uses that time for Black college tours. Her ultimate goal is for her son to attend Morehouse. She's already taken him to Morehouse at the age of nine and was able to schedule an hour meeting with the admissions officer. Everyone is in agreement that his objective, nine years later, is to be a freshman at Morehouse College. She hangs pictures in his bedroom of Morehouse. She uses them as a reminder and motivational tool whenever her son begins to slack off on his work.

I have described an ideal picture, of course, and the reality is that while the number of children being home-schooled is increasing, there are more than 9 million African American children taking their chances each day in public schools.

One of the solutions, that we recommend in this book, involves participation by the approximately four million African

Americans who have earned a college degree. No other country in the world has as many Black people with degrees as the United States. There are more Africans in Nigeria, South Africa, Ghana, and Brazil, but no group is better educated than African Americans. As the late Carter G. Woodson, author of *The Mis-education of the Negro*, said in his best seller of 1933, educated to do what? Educated to work for whom?

I'm challenging the four million African Americans with degrees to consider teaching for a minimum of one year. The program could be called Teach for America. If that commitment is not possible on a full-time basis, then my next challenge would be to volunteer at an inner-city school, ideally once a week, at least once a month. If even that is not possible, consider becoming a tutor at a community organization or church. Our nine million children need to be beneficiaries of the four million African Americans with higher education.

Our next solution comes from Education Trust. They have documented that the major variable in academic achievement is not the income of the family, its marital status, or the parents' educational attainment or involvement; the key factors are the qualifications and commitment of the teachers. The Trust has identified four major variables: the teacher's GPA, major, proficiency on the state exam, and their students' academic performance. They identified 4,500 high-poverty and/or high-minority schools that scored in the top one-third of all schools nationwide. The following graphs document the fact that the most important factor in education is the classroom teacher.

# Education

## The Effect of Different Teachers On Low-Achieving Students Tennessee

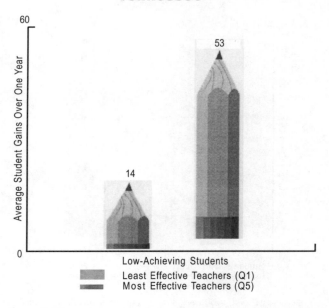

Sanders, William L. and Rivers, Joan C. "Cumulative And Residual Effects of Teachers on Future Student Academic Achievement."

## Cumulative Effects of Teacher Sequence on Fifth Grade Math Scores: Tennessee

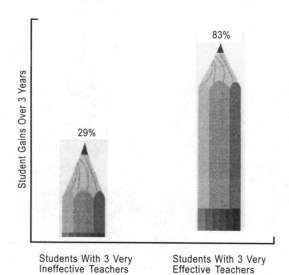

Sanders, William L. and Rivers, Joan C. "Cumulative And Residual Effects of Teachers on Future Student Academic Achievement."

# Education

## Effects On Students' Reading Scores In Dallas (Grades 4-6)

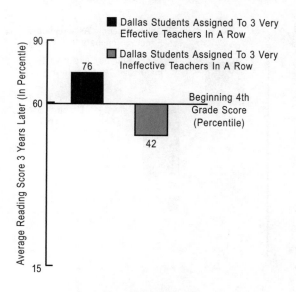

Source: Heather Jordan, Robert Mendro, & Dash Weerasinghe, "Teacher Effects On Longitudinal Student Achievement" 1997.

## Effects On Students' Math
## Scores In Dallas (Grades 3-5)

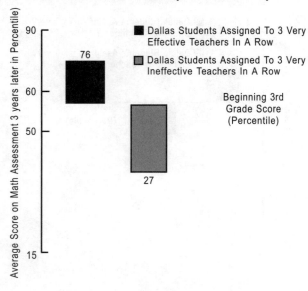

Source: Heather Jordan, Robert Mendro, & Dash Weerasinghe,
"Teacher Effects On Longitudinal Student Achievement" 1997.

# Education

## Boston Students With Effective Teachers Showed Greater Gains

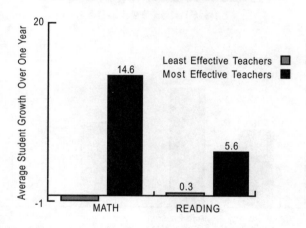

Source: Boston Public Schools, "High School Restructuring," March 9, 1998.

**Percentage of Classes Taught By
Teachers Lacking A Major
In Field, 1993-94**

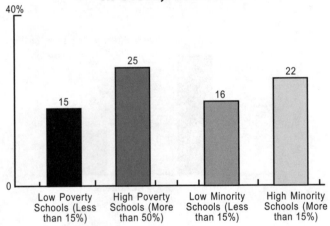

Source: Richard Ingersoll, University of Georgia, Unpublished,
1998.

# Education

## African American Students Are More Likely To Have Underqualified Teachers: Tennessee

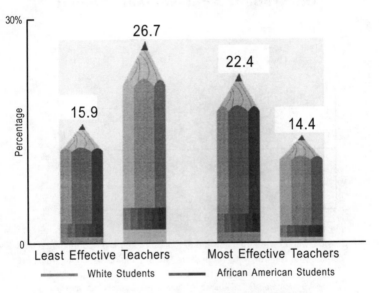

Source: Sanders, William L. and Rivers, Joan C. "Cumulative And Residual Effects of Teachers on Future Student Academic Achievement."

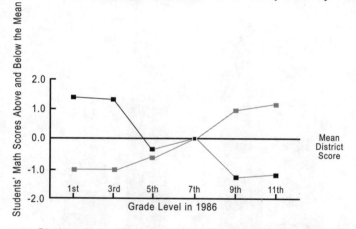

## Long-Range Effects
## Of Low-Scoring and High-Scoring Teachers
## On Student Achievement (Texas)

Students' Math Scores Above and Below the Mean

Grade Level in 1986

Mean District Score

- Districts with Low-Scoring 1st and 3rd Graders and High-Scoring Teachers
- Districts with High Scoring 1st and 3rd Graders and Low-Scoring Teachers

Source: Ronald F. Ferguson, "Evidence That Schools Can Narrow the Black-White Test Score Gap," 1997.

70

# Education

I have categorized teachers into five areas:
1. Custodians
2. Referral Agents
3. Instructors
4. Teachers
5. Coaches

Unfortunately, in many African American schools, there is a shortage of teachers and coaches and an excessive number of custodians, referral agents, and instructors.

Custodians are educators who use the same lesson plans every year. They make derogatory comments about African American children and are quick to say, "I have mine and you have yours to get" They remind anyone who will listen how many days, weeks, and months they have before retirement.

Referral agents don't educate children; they refer them. Research shows that 20 percent of the teachers make 80 percent of the referrals. Isn't it ironic that with a coach or a teacher, the child is not often recommended for special education placement, but with a referral agent, unfortunately, is placed?

Instructors honestly admit that they teach subjects, not students. You will hear them say that they teach reading, math, or history—and they mean just that. I've learned from researching the education of African American children that there can be no significant learning until there is first a significant relationship.

Teachers not only understand subject matter, but they also understand that there should be a congruence between pedagogy and learning styles. They realize that you do not give left-brained lesson plans to right-brained-thinking children. They realize that children learn in different ways.

Coaches understand both subject matter and pedagogy, but more importantly they bond with students. They realize that you cannot teach a child without love, respect, and an understanding of their culture.

I also recommend looping teachers. This provides the opportunity for a master teacher or coach to stay with his or her children for several years. Numerous teachers have told me that they did not want to give their children up to a subsequent teacher after the great accomplishments they had achieved. Unfortunately, many African American students have experienced the "volley ball" effect. They have a master teacher for one grade, but a custodian, referral agent, or instructor follows. Looping allows master teachers and coaches to stay with their children for several years. I don't recommend looping custodians, referral agents, and instructors.

The parallel solution is serial teaching. In many schools there are several classes per grade. Many master teachers and coaches arrange with their principals for their children to go on to an ear-marked classroom for the following grade. This allows children to experience master teachers consecutively.

The Heritage Foundation has released an excellent book by Samuel Casey Carter, entitled *No Excuses: Lessons from 21 High Performing, High Poverty Schools.* Education Trust identified 4,500 schools in low-income areas nationwide that scored in the top third of their state. Carter's high-performing, high-poverty schools have several similarities. The most important person in the equation is the principal. All the research shows that the principal makes the difference. Unfortunately, there are many principals who have become CEOs of their building and choose to remain in their office, monitoring the budget and maintaining the facility. More effective principals become the instructional leaders of their building. They walk corridors, visit classrooms, give teachers suggestions, and create opportunities for referral agents, custodians, and instructors to observe master teachers and coaches. They have created an environment in the school where both students and teachers believe that learning is going to take place.

Such principals employ teachers who have high expectations of their children. Masters of time on task, they are very selective about what takes place during instructional time and will do whatever is necessary to make that time count. There are few if any messages over the intercom or assemblies during the first three hours of the school day. These principals are not afraid of tests and realize that America is a test-taking country. They are very clear about this testing reality, whether it's third or eighth grade, high school, college admission, graduation exams, or licenses for medicine, law, accounting, and real estate. They also understand how they can relax children by using tests for diagnostic purposes. The more frequently children test, the more comfortable they become.

One of the major concerns in the African American community is the issue of high-stakes testing. I have worked with numerous states and communities on this issue. There is a tremendous schism, not only in the country, but also within the African American community, over high-stakes testing. Approximately 20 states have implemented high-stakes testing. Earlier, in the chapter we mentioned that the average twelfth-grade African American is performing at the level of the average eighth-grade white student. Employers need to be assured that when they hire a high school graduate, that employee has twelfth-grade reading and math capability.

Let me cite Florida as an example. The NAACP has filed a lawsuit against the state for the miseducation of our children.

The state mandated that a test, called the FCAT, be given to all children in grades three, eight, and twelve.

Seventy-three percent of White students passed the FCAT. Fifty-one percent of Hispanics and only 41 percent of African Americans passed. There's no question that it is unfair to students for them to be retained in third, eighth, and twelfth grades in schools filled with custodians, referral agents, and instructors, where the roof leaks, the furnace works improperly, and air condition is nonexistent. It is also unfair when one school district receives $15,000 to $20,000 per child annually and another school district in the same state receives $4,000 to $6,000 per child.

How do we explain, though, the testing disparity when the children attend the same school? The answer could lie in factors that were mentioned in the chapter "Integration Revisited." Schools can look integrated on the outside, but can be highly segregated internally because of tracking. In addition, students can be integrated within the school, but the teachers' expectations are skewed based on race. Furthermore, schools can be integrated while the curriculum remains Eurocentric and the pedagogy continues to be left-brain oriented.

Albeit, we need to ask ourselves, "Could our scores have been improved if we had studied and practiced taking tests more frequently? If we had spent less time watching television, listening to rap, and playing?" I believe that every church, community organization, and school within the African American community needs to open its doors after hours and on weekends to provide our children with test-taking skills.

The next solution is the Comer School Development Program. It was founded in 1968 by James Comer. He realized that with the breakdown of the village, children needed better support systems. The Comer Model is based on collaboration, consensus, and no-fault. There are three teams, one each focused on management, student and staff support, and parents. Every decision is child-centered and parents are on all teams.

The program started in two schools in Hartford, Connecticut, and has grown to include more than 500 schools in 21 states. The three goals are to improve parental involvement, increase attendance, and upgrade test scores. All of which have been accomplished. For example, Gompers Elementary School in Detroit was in the poorest school district, but achieved the highest test scores in the state, using the Comer Model.

The following solution comes from KIPP (Knowledge Is Power Program). The KIPP Academy began in 1994 in Houston, Texas. Michael Feinberg and David Levin were two novice, frustrated Houston teachers who did not believe what they heard in the teachers' lounge: that low-income African American and Hispanic children from single-parent homes could not learn. These two teachers believed that the kids simply needed more time on task. They negotiated with their principal to stay an extra hour after school, and before the year concluded, they witnessed a tremendous improvement in their children's test scores.

Feinberg and Levin then negotiated with the Houston superintendent to form a school of only master teachers who were willing to work extra hours during the week, three to four hours on Saturday, and give up half of their summer vacations. Test scores soared.

The KIPP Academy now has over 20 charter schools nationwide. A major component of KIPP's success is greater time on task. This is reinforced by the SAT scores I mentioned earlier. Contrary to Charles Murray's belief, stated in his book *The Bell Curve* that the reason for the academic gap is genetically driven, the reality is that Asians average 1083 on the SAT because they study 12 hours per week. Whites score

1063 because they study eight hours a week. Hispanics score 903 because they study five hours per week. African Americans score 857 because they only study four hours per week. When I ask African American students nationwide how many hours they study, many of them say less than one hour per week.

For the past decade we have been trying to implement single-gender classrooms and single-gender schools. In the private sector, there are thousands of single-gender schools. Unfortunately, 91 percent of African American children attend public schools. The challenge has been Title 9 legislation and organizations such as the ACLU (American Civil Liberties Union) and NOW (National Organization for Women). When we tried to implement these schools in Detroit—Marcus Garvey, Malcolm X, and Paul Robeson—we lost in court because the judge ruled that it violated Title 9 gender-equity legislation.

During the 1990s, numerous principals implemented single-gender classrooms. Often the media were not aware of these classes. In Seattle, Washington, the Thurgood Marshall Elementary School implemented single-gender classrooms, because the principal was very frustrated that 80 percent of his suspensions consisted of male students, and his males scored only at the 16th percentile on the state achievement tests.

After implementing single-gender classrooms, suspensions dropped by 78 percent, and his male students' test scores improved to the 73rd percentile. We have seen similar improvements replicated nationwide. The federal education department and the judicial system are now willing to reconsider single-gender classrooms in public schools as long as what is provided for males is provided for females.

The research also shows that girls benefit greatly from single-gender classrooms, specifically in their pursuit of math and science careers. In addition to improved test scores and graduation rates, there is a decrease in the dropout rate and pregnancy. I encourage you to pursue more research online from the National Association for Single Sex Public Education.

Over the past decade, I have conducted quarterly Black male conferences because, unfortunately, most educators never received a course in college on male learning styles. I believe that many schools are using a female pedagogy with large numbers of male students. Even White males are placed in special education and remedial classes in far greater numbers than White females.

Theoretically and practically, teachers know that boys have a shorter attention span, less verbal competency, higher energy level, and more advanced gross motor activity than females and are less mature and poorer listeners. The problem has been trying to convince teachers that if boys have a shorter attention span, the lesson plans need to be shortened. Because of their greater energy, more movement should be allowed. More objects and artifacts should be provided for those more active gross motor needs. Because of the difference in maturation, we should avoid comparing boys to girls, and if boys do not listen as well, they need to sit in the front of the classroom.

Given that girls have 20 percent more nerve tissue connecting the right and left hemispheres of the brain, we should understand why they have greater ability in language arts. I recommend that every teacher attend one of these conferences or immerse themselves in the literature regarding male and female learning styles.

Unfortunately, people seem to feel that if you're different from them, you're deficient from them. In Europe, where they have more male teachers, girls are placed in special education in greater numbers. In America, where we have more female teachers, boys are placed in special education in greater numbers. The same demon driving racism also fuels sexism.

I repeat, have we unwittingly designed female classrooms for large numbers of male students?

Since 1972, the Council of Independent Black Institutions (CIBI) has been effectively educating African American children using the combination of an Africentric curriculum, high expectations, and a full understanding of their learning styles. Asa Hilliard makes the excellent point in his book *Young, Gifted, and Black* that too many times when we talk about the achievement gap, we use White students as the benchmark and barometer. We have allowed ourselves to pursue the discussion comparing White and Black students on the basis of White students representing the best and the standard. When we talk about the gap, let's talk about the gap between African American students in an under-performing public school and African American students in CIBI schools.

If we confine discussion of the learning gap purely to race, it becomes inevitable that we question innate ability. Rather, we should point out that CIBI children, also from low-income single-parent homes, are at the 90th percentile or better in reading and math while children in the same neighborhood who attend public schools are at the second or third stanine on the same test?

The difference in performance is the result of what CIBI offers: Africentricity, Nguzo Saba, Ma'at, (African value systems) high expectations, an understanding of African American children's learning styles, and creation of a village comprising home, school, and community. The historical challenge for CIBI schools has been economics. Many of the parents have had difficulty paying the tuition needed to adequately pay CIBI teachers. Many of my friends are CIBI administrators. Their challenge historically has been trying to secure staff to teach their children. Interestingly, many of their staff members have not completed college degrees, but because of their commitment and understanding of our children's learning styles, have produced excellent results.

I'm glad that when the Education Trust looked at the components for evaluating a master teacher, they allowed historical track records to be considered. One emerging trend is that some CIBI schools have become charter schools. On the other hand, many parents who couldn't afford the tuition opted to take their children out of CIBI schools and put them into African-immersion charter schools. This has created some internal concerns for CIBI.

How can Black colleges with only 16 percent of the Black students nationally produce more than 30 percent of the graduates? Some who are suffering from racism would say that it's easier to graduate from a Black college. If that were true, how do we explain that 75 percent of African American undergraduates of Black colleges go on to receive graduate degrees from White universities?

Many are unaware that the school that has the largest number of African American National Merit Scholars is not Harvard, Yale, or Princeton. It's Florida A&M University. The school that has the greatest percentage placement of its graduates in medical and dental school is Xavier University. When Fortune 500 companies are looking for the best African American engineers, they know to visit North Carolina A&T. When Wall Street is looking for African Americans in business, they know to consider Florida A&M and Howard University.

Some schools will admit you and other schools will help you to graduate. I speak at about 60 colleges annually. One of their major concerns is retention. Unfortunately, the retention rate for African American students hovers around 32 percent. There are schools, White and Black, where the retention is between 60 and 80 percent. Every African American student before they enter college needs to find out what the retention rate is at each university they are interested in. It is suicidal for an African American student to enter a school with a retention rate below 50 percent.

In the "Integration Revisited" chapter, we talked about the contradiction of wanting integration while also wanting to maintain Black colleges. As a result, many of our Black colleges have an increasing percentage of White students and White faculty. Unfortunately, many Black colleges also have closed or are having major fiscal problems.

African Americans need to increase their support of the United Negro College Fund (UNCF). How can a people earn $688 billion and point with pride to almost four million African American graduates, yet not be able to support Black students who are seeking college degrees? I'm appealing to everyone reading this book and all of Black America to put UNCF on their Christmas list. Everyone should make a contribution. It concerns me that we want entertainers and athletes to finance our movement when the reality is that if 36 million Black people each gave just one dollar, it would amount to $36 million. We could liquidate the debt of Morris Brown in the bat of an eye.

Because this book is solution oriented, we need to give kudos to Tom Joyner and his foundation that gave $1 million to Morris Brown and has given tens of millions of dollars to Black colleges and Black students. Tom Joyner is another reminder to all the nay sayers who whine, "What can I do? I'm only one person."

Another solution is Saturday Academies. Two of the finest are my own African American Images Talent Center in Chicago and the W.E.B. DuBois Learning Center in Kansas City, Missouri. There are organizations who unlike CIBI, do not create full-time schools, but have a tremendous commitment to our children and have chosen weekdays or weekends to make a difference in their lives. These Saturday Academies include the traditional academic subjects, but also provide

# Education

Africentricity, martial arts, and fine arts. Numerous organizations have found success by teaching youth to play chess. Research has shown it has improved test scores, increased attention span, reduced disciplinary problems, and developed critical thinking skills. I recommended every youth program to incorporate chess into their curriculum.

It's no accident that 84 percent of the NBA is African American and that popular music is also dominated by African Americans. In the Black community, if you want to become an engineer, if you want to pursue math and science, if you want to improve your academic performance, where can you go? These Saturday Academies are shining examples of what can be done when men and women pool their resources and value academics.

Saturday Academies teach Africentricity, the Nguzo Saba, and Ma'at. Carter G. Woodson's *The Mis-education of the Negro* asks what benefit is an African American with a college degree and no commitment to the race? If our best Black minds do not live, work, spend, invest, and/or volunteer in the Black community, can it be anything else but a ghetto? It is very difficult to reeducate an adult who has been taught from a Eurocentric perspective. Saturday Academies illustrate that it's much easier to educate children to appreciate their history and culture than to expect Clarence Thomas to become Africentric.

An excellent example of organizations trying to make a difference are the NAACP and the African Academic Cultural Technological and Science Olympics (ACT-SO). Over the past two decades, under the leadership of Vernon Jarrett and numerous others, they host local, regional, and national conferences to showcase African American youth, outside of sports, who have done well academically.

Saturday Academies remind me of what Jews do in their synagogues. If Jewish parents send their children to public schools, it is only for reading, writing, and arithmetic. They use the synagogue after school and weekends to make sure their children understand what happened in Nazi Germany and the importance of Israel, their faith, and their culture.

Many of the Saturday Academies, CIBI, charter schools, progressive public schools, and home-schoolers use African American Images' curriculum, SETCLAE (Self-Esteem Through Culture Leads To Academic Excellence). This is an African American, multicultural K-12 curriculum with workbooks and textbooks for each grade.

I never will forget my good friend Dr. Folami Prescott Adams, who challenged me in 1988 after hearing me speak. She asked me if I really believed that teachers were going to return to their schools and develop Africentric lesson plans based on the information I had given them? I said that 10 to 20 percent would, but I agreed that the majority of teachers would not. I then challenged her and asked if she'd be willing to work with me on developing lesson plans that teachers could use from kindergarten through twelfth grade. Six months later we completed those lesson plans, and SETCLAE has now been used in more than 5,000 schools and academies nationwide.

I also want to commend the National Association of Black School Educators (NABSE) for creating a pre-referral intervention guide, addressing the over-representation of African American students in special education. If a school has a 17 percent African American population, then they should not exceed that percentage in special education.

# Education

I also recommend that before another child in America receives Ritalin or is placed in special education, the following be considered:

1. Reduction in sugar consumption
2. Reduction in television viewing
3. Ear, eye, and thyroid gland exams
4. Allergy tests
5. Elimination of food additives, especially MSG and BHT
6. Hypoglycemia test
7. Examination for mineral, vitamin, and nutrient deficiency
8. More right-brain lesson plans
9. Examination of the curriculum for cultural relevancy
10. Consideration of teacher change
11. Implementation of cooperative learning
12. Provide greater student attention
13. Consideration of single-gender classrooms

We must teach African American children how to succeed academically. Some of the lessons we learn from coaches in the athletic arena can be transferred to the classroom. The Efficacy Program founded by Jeff Howard in Boston should be adopted by all schools. The four major attributes of the psychology of performance are ability, effort, luck, and the nature of the task.

When students have strong self-esteem, they attribute their success to either their ability or effort. When such a student earns 100 on a test, they will tell themselves that they are good in math, or they studied hard and that's why they earned the 100. If the same student did poorly on the math test, they would attribute their failure to lack of effort. Because the failure is attributed to lack of effort, they are in control of correcting their problem by increasing their study time for the next test.

Unfortunately, those students with low self-esteem who receive 100 on a particular test will say that the test was easy or it was luck. If they do poorly on the test, they attribute it to their lack of ability. When they make that critical mistake of questioning their ability, they are no longer in control. Therefore, there is no longer a need to study harder the next time; they have convinced themselves that they are not good in that particular subject.

The Minority Student Achievement Network (MSAN) was created to address the under-performance of African Americans in affluent communities like Berkeley, CA, Evanston, IL, Ann Arbor, MI, Cambridge, MA, and Shaker and Cleveland Heights, OH. Middle-class African American parents cannot make the mistake of trusting their children to a school district because they live in an affluent community and then focus on working long hours to pay for their mortgage and Mercedes. They must monitor teachers, abolish tracking, demand more African American teachers, have greater expectations, and acquire a better understanding of African American learning styles. Parents must actively involve themselves in their children's homework. They must teach their children Rule 110.

I strongly encourage every school to adopt the MAC scholar program (Minority Achievement Committee) founded in Shaker Heights, Ohio in 1990. High Achieving, upper class high school students mentor freshmen to improve their grades and dispel being smart is acting White. This is an excellent utilization of positive peer pressure.

Let's now look at the next chapter on solutions for the Black family.

# CHAPTER 5

# FAMILY AND HEALTH

There are approximately nine million African American families. The U.S. Census reports there are 36 million African Americans. They also report that 48 percent of African American families are headed by couples, which represents a 520,000 increase over the past six years. The media has been silent about this increase. They love talking about the large number of African American single-parent families. The good news that has gone unreported has been the steady increase in the number of families headed by couples. Almost half of African American families are headed by couples.

The media has also been silent about the fact that 9 percent of African American families are led by African American single males, which translates into approximately 810,000 African American male single parents. It would be nice if every once in a while the networks on their nightly news broadcast, before they talk about the last murder or drug deal gone bad, would show an African American father braiding his daughter's hair in preparation for school the next day. The major objective of this book is to accentuate the positive.

There has also been a decline in the percentage of households that are led by single females, which includes mothers, grandmothers, and aunts. Over the past five years, there has been a 5 percent decline in the percentage of African American families headed by mothers. Again, the media has been silent. Forty-three percent of African American families are headed by females. The reality is that more African American families are led by couples than by single-parent mothers or fathers.

There is a difference, though, between the percentage of families led by couples and the percentage of children who have both mothers and fathers in the home. There are families only populated by spouses. There are families with several children and only one parent, sometimes the grandparent. The statistical reality is that while 48 percent of African American families are headed by couples, unfortunately almost 68 percent of African American children are in single-parent homes.

In my earlier book *State of Emergency: We Must Save African American Males*, I discuss five types of fathers in Black America. They include Sperm Donors, No Show Daddies, Ice Cream Daddies, Stepfathers, and Daddies. Unfortunately, in the African American community we have far too many Sperm Donors. They stay less than 18 seconds in contrast to Daddies, who never leave.

No Show Daddies are those who promise they're going to pick their children up for an outing on Monday, but on Saturday, unfortunately, are no shows. Can we blame this behavior on the White man?

Ice Cream Daddies do show up, buy their children lots of ice cream, and take them to sporting events and other social activities. Unfortunately, they don't feel the need to check homework, assign chores, and make their kids eat nutritiously.

The next group are Stepfathers. In European culture, which is hierarchical in nature, there is a tremendous desire to compare rank. The biological father is given the honor of being called father while the residential father who stays around is called stepfather. This is purely a European phenomenon. In African culture, we believe in the extended family: you simply have two fathers, biological and residential, but not step. In addition, how can we label the father "step" when he stays, pays bills, helps with homework, and puts food on the table?

# Family and Health

The last group are Daddies. In addition to the 810,000 single-parent fathers, there are approximately two million African American fathers who stay with their wives and children.

In the past, the men of the community visited any young man who had impregnated a young woman in their community. We need to return to that concept, which is similar to that espoused by MAD DADS and will be discussed in a later chapter. I want to call this group Village Fathers. We need all positive men to affiliate as Village Fathers in their neighborhoods. This group will visit sperm donors and offer parenting and career development counseling.

### Africa 1604

A teenage boy wants to marry his girlfriend. He asks the girl's parents for permission. Her parents discuss the matter with his parents. After much deliberation among the parents and their children, consent is given. The ceremony includes the entire village.

### America 2004

A teenage boy has sex with his girlfriend. She becomes pregnant. She is afraid to tell her single-parent mother and considers abortion. Her mother finds out she is pregnant, refuses to consider abortion, and is furious with the unemployed, illiterate boy who is now dating someone else.

One of the challenges we discussed in "Integration Revisited" is that the village is not as strong in the new millennium as it was before 1954. In that era, the brother or sister with a PhD lived on the same block with the brother or sister on ADC. Now, there is a widening gap between the

Black haves and the Black have nots. Often in mentoring programs, the mentors live in the suburbs while the mentees live in the inner city. Thus, there is a tremendous need for mentoring if for no other reason than mentees no longer have the luxury and privilege of observing positive mentors.

In my book *State of Emergency*, I indicated that as significant as racism and poverty are, the greatest problem facing the African American community is fatherlessness. What can we do about the 68 percent of our children living in fatherless households? We need to marshal our 85,000 churches, four million college graduates, $688 billion, and 102 Black colleges to solve this dilemma. We need Village Fathers to speak up in locker rooms and barbershops, where brothers brag about the number of women they have and the number of babies made.

We need Village Fathers, in the spirit of love and wisdom, to share phrases such as:

"Boys prefer quantity and men value quality."

"When you find the right one there is no need for more."

"Real men would not expect another man or the government to take care of their children."

"Do you want someone treating your daughter, sister, or mother the way you are treating her."

I strongly recommend that men struggling with becoming a father contact Charles Ballard and the Institute for Responsible Fatherhood. They will assist you in employment, parenting, custody, and improving your relationship with your child's mother. Ballard believes many parenting issues could be resolved if there were reconciliation between adults.

Rev. Jesse Lee Peterson is the founder of BOND (Brotherhood Organization of a New Destiny). The program founded in 1990 helps troubled young men make the full

# Family and Health

transition into manhood. BOND provides shelter, character development, education, and economic literacy.

Excellent organizations that have done great work in this area are the Urban League and the Alpha Phi Alpha fraternity. The Urban League's Male Responsibility Project needs to be continued. They ran a media campaign with excellent billboards and magazine advertisements that reinforced the importance of males in the lives of children. The fraternity's program is Project Alpha. Unfortunately, most teen pregnancy programs counsel girls and continue the absurd philosophy that boys will be boys. They will be if you allow it. We need to begin to hold them responsible. It is ridiculous that 90 percent of teen pregnancy programs counsel females and exempt males when each has a 50-50 responsibility. I challenge all fraternities to step up to the plate and create programs that will teach male responsibility, and please do not assume I am an Alpha. We were Africans before Greeks.

Forty-three percent of our families are led by single females, and some mothers make the critical mistake of making derogatory comments about their child's father in the child's presence. Many children defend the absent parent. Proverbs 18:21 says, "Death and life are in the power of the tongue." Satan lied when he said sticks and stones may break your bones, but words will never hurt you.

It is impossible for a man to be a pimp without a whore. African American men and women have much more in common than they have in opposition. The problem lies not exclusively with Black men. Women and men mirror each other. At the gut level, opposites do not attract. Can you imagine 10 million African American women telling their men that there will be no more sex outside of marriage? Marriage would increase. I believe men know which woman will accept abuse.

It is unfortunate that African American men do not realize that the same demon that drives racism drives sexism. It is an obsession with power. It is the rationale that because someone is different from you, they are deficient and inferior. African American men can see the speck of racism in the White man's eye, but can't see the log of sexism in their own eye. There is almost an oath of silence in the Black community about rape, wife abuse, and incest.

The same applies in the larger society with the feminization of poverty. While the lack of male presence is significant, what may be just as significant is the lack of male income. When the man and woman were together, he made $18 per hour and she made $9 per hour, together a total of $27 per hour. That income was adequate for raising their family, but if they separate or divorce (66 percent divorce rate in the African American community, 50 percent in the White community), the reality is that the woman is now responsible for raising children on a $9 per hour salary. This is the feminization of poverty. It is ridiculous for a janitor or prison guard without a college degree to earn more than a degreed teacher.

Noted psychiatrist, Frances Welsing has recommended for the past two decades the numbers 28, 30, 2, and 4. She suggests that we do not marry until we first master self-esteem. When many people divorce, they comment that the other person did not make them happy. Apparently, they transferred their happiness and joy to another person, which is an error. Dr. Welsing feels that it may take until a person is 28 years of age to fully understand that they are responsible for their own happiness. When I've shared this theory with an audience, people want to argue and nitpick about the numbers. The numbers are not as important as the concept. If you feel you

# Family and Health

have mastered self at 16 years of age (and truly have), then you're eligible for marriage. We need to be honest in understanding the importance of self before moving to the second level of unity, which is family. In math one-half plus one-half equals one, but in relationships two incomplete people equal one-half and will make each other miserable.

The second number Dr. Welsing recommends is 30, the minimum age for having children. She feels that before we have children, we need to discuss child rearing. We need to learn about each other and appreciate each other and, if at all possible, travel and experience the joys of marriage before parenting. There's nothing worse than to find out after the fact that one believes in the discipline of "time out" and the other values the belt.

The third number represents the number of children. People in my audiences have argued about that number. Welsing simply feels you should not bring into the world children that you cannot adequately nurture. It's interesting that those who have the most financially often have the fewest children. Those who have the least financially, often have the most. I would encourage you to read *The Jewish Phenomenon* to gain a better understanding of how the Jews utilized their resources to maximize their potential.

Lastly, Welsing recommends the number four. You should space children four years apart. In her practice as a psychiatrist, she has observed that many children do not receive enough lap time and nurturance. Some families have babies every nine months. When children do not receive enough lap time, nursing, and nurturance, they are tremendously desirous of attention. This can be expressed in numerous negative behaviors.

Unfortunately, in the African American community, our present numbers are 0, 13, 9, and 1. We are not getting married.

Children are being born to girls no older than 13 and we're often having nine children at one-year intervals. Those are not the numbers we need to build a nation. Nation building numbers are closer to 28, 30, 2, and 4.

There are 291 million Americans today and 54 million have a sexually transmitted disease (STD). If you exclude children under 11 and seniors over 80, the numbers affected are at epidemic proportions. Twenty-five percent of all teens have a STD. Teen pregnancy has declined while STDs have increased.

When Bill Clinton made his infamous statement, "I did not have sex with that woman," many youth took him literally and now have defined oral sex as outside sexual precincts. They naively believe they are virgins although participating in oral sex. What has flabbergasted me in workshops with youth and adults is how someone can define himself or herself as a virgin, while being infected with syphilis, chlamydia, or gonorrhea or, unfortunately, are HIV positive. **Oral sex is sex,** and AIDS has now usurped homicide as the number one killer in Black America.

The other challenge here is that if you monitor television shows, you will find that less than 10 percent (and I'm being generous; some reports have said less than 1 percent) of the sex portrayed involves spouses. How unfortunate that the media is a major purveyor of promiscuity.

The good news—because that's the objective of this book—is that there are many excellent abstinence programs. For example, there is a great program called "It's Not Worth It" that was created by former basketball star A.C. Green. I strongly recommend that every church, community organization, and school utilize some abstinence program, particularly A.C. Green's. It's a reflection of our own low expectations to believe that the best way to teach children sex education is by omitting abstinence and going straight to condom distribution. If that's our best strategy, remember that condom efficacy is only 87 percent, and that's if it's used correctly.

Our youth deserve a better strategy. Young people often say that no one taught them abstinence. In teenage sex education classes, we must talk not only about abstinence, but also about the media, which includes television and music. We need to help young people gain a better understanding of the impact that videos, music, and television shows have on their sexual behavior. They need to be exposed to young people who have taken an oath of abstinence and have been successful for years. I encourage you to watch the powerful video and read the report released by MEE Productions, This is My Reality: The Price of Sex—An Inside look at Black Urban Youth Sexuality and the Role of Media.

One of the major concerns that we must address is the high incidence of AIDS. African Americans represent only 12 percent of the U.S. population, but Black males constitute 43 percent of male AIDS victims. African American women constitute 64 percent of female AIDS victims. There's a 1 percent chance that a patient was infected because of a bad blood transfusion and a 38 percent chance that it was due to drug usage. The largest possibility is through sexual transmission.

Unfortunately, there are many men who are living "down under"; they have not been honest with their women and have infected them. Satan no longer wears a black or red T-shirt and hat. Many of these men who infect their women are pastors, teachers, athletes, police officers, doctors, lawyers, firemen, and other professionals, many of them homosexual. You'd think if someone is married with children and in a macho career, he would not be homosexual. Often, the career is simply a cover up.

Bisexuality is running rampant in the African American community. Shahrazad Ali has written an excellent book, *How to Tell If Your Man Is Gay or Bisexual*, to help all women, but especially African American females, decipher the signs in their men before they play Russian roulette with their lives. She describes the following telltale signs:

1. Men are very territorial. If another man enters his space or violates his square, he'll move away or take a step back. If he doesn't move, this might be a sign that he's open to getting closer.
2. He's effeminate. Some men slowly move into a feminine stance or pose.
3. He holds eye contact too long with a man, or he holds on to the other's hand after shaking it.
4. He watches other men a little too much.
5. Check out his friends.
6. How does he sleep at night? What position does he sleep in? Does he sleep like a woman or a man? What does he talk about in his sleep?
7. Has he been single just a bit too long? What is his history with women?
8. Discuss homosexuality with him.
9. Discuss child molestation with him.
10. Touch his rectum to see if he has those telltale bumps on his anus from having it stretched by a penis.
11. Check his underwear for tiny streaks of bloodstains.
12. Chart his sex life. How often are you and he intimate? Are you always the one who has to start the process rolling?
13. Does he have a lot of unexplained absences?
14. Does he like anal stimulation?
15. Does he like to have anal sex more than vaginal sex?
16. Some women get their gay friend to hit on their man to determine his response.[12]

# Family and Health

Another clear illustration of sexism is for men who know they are HIV positive to irresponsibly infect their wives or women who care about them.

Thirty-eight percent of HIV infections are drug related. In Europe they do not use the penal system to solve their drug problem. They believe drug treatment is essential. They allocate one-third of what we spend per inmate on addicts. Only 1 percent of their drug users are HIV positive in contrast to America, where more than 60 percent of intravenous drug users are HIV positive. In Europe, they realize that needles should not be shared and should not be obtained in back alleys. As a result, drug users can go to a clinic and receive clean needles. In a later chapter on churches, we will look at successful models that have gone beyond the European approach and have demonstrated greater success by introducing addicts to the blood of Jesus.

How do we reduce the 66 percent divorce rate in the African American community? One of the things that we must do is make a distinction between love and lust. Cece Winans mentioned that love is the result of first being loved by Jesus and that people who are not in love with God are not able to give love to another person. Often a person in lust will say, "I love you because you make me feel good." If you stop making them feel good, the lust will go away. There's a tremendous distinction between love and lust. Love is giving; lust is taking. Love is spiritual; lust is physical. *Love is a decision not a feeling.*

There are four stages in a relationship:
1. selection
2. romance
3. problem
4. commitment

In several of my earlier books, I discuss the above in more detail. There is a science to selecting the right mate. Many people blow it in stage one. We all love the romantic stage, but invariably whoever you're with you will experience problems. The only way to reach the commitment stage is to *work* through the problems. Research shows those couples who endured the problems experienced better marriages five years later. Unfortunately, those who divorced bailed out early and did not stay long enough to experience God's blessings.

Another distinction is between friend and lover. In the physical society in which we live, unfortunately, most people marry their lovers. We belittle friendship with statements like, "There's nothing going on. We're just friends." Yet, the major reason for divorce is the lack of communication. We could reduce divorce in America if we emphasized friendship more. I'm very happy that Smokey Robinson has given his life to Jesus Christ and has begun to sing gospel music. During the remaining years of his career, he'll have to make a critical decision about how many songs he will sing about lust in comparison to the love songs that come from the gospel.

It is unfortunate to admit that the divorce rate in the church is almost as high as the divorce rate in the world. Note that I said the divorce rate in the church. I did not say the divorce rate in Christ. There is a distinction between being in church and being in Christ. There are people who have their weddings in church, but are not members of the church. I often wonder why they bothered to have their wedding in the church and why the pastor allowed it. Was it for financial reasons? Was it simply because the couple asked?

Where a couple is married is very important. There are implications when a person chooses to be married in a church, a lounge, a college, a cruise ship, a casino, or City Hall. A preview of the marriage can be determined by the location of the wedding. I'm also concerned about churches that marry couples without premarital counseling. There are numerous churches that have an excellent success rate with their couples, because they provide extensive premarital counseling. One of the significant factors that determines their success is setting the wedding date only after successful counseling. It is a contradiction for a couple to receive a date before they have successfully matriculated in premarital counseling. It becomes almost a joke if you're given a date while you're still in counseling. It belittles the sessions. Couples respect premarital counseling far more when they know that their date is contingent upon successful matriculation.

Those churches with a high success rate also provide continual marriage enrichment. As demanding as careers and child rearing are, even more demanding is your marriage. It's unfortunate that so many couples spend thousands of dollars on the wedding and honeymoon, but won't spend $10 for a book, audio, or video cassette on how to strengthen their marriage.

Earlier, I made the distinction between being in church and being in Christ. When Jesus said put the house on the rock, He meant on Him, not on a building. A building won't keep the marriage together, but a personal relationship with Jesus Christ will.

My pastor, Bill Winston, has taught me the importance of words. Proverbs 18:21 says, "Death and life are in the power of the tongue." Hebrews 11:3 says, "God framed the world by His words." Pastor Winston shared with us, in a marriage enrichment class, that there was a time early in his marriage where he and his wife were having some problems. He began making negative comments, until the Lord reminded him of the importance of words. He then developed a confession of faith that described her beauty, intellect, spirituality, and acumen as a mother, homemaker, and lover. Two things happened as he continued to make this daily confession. First, his outlook toward his wife changed. He began to see her through a different prism. His entire worldview was changed by his confession. Second, she became what he confessed, and now he claims that he has one of the best marriages any man could have, all as a result of his confession of faith.

I'd also like to discuss child rearing. Reginald Clark, in the book *Family Life and School Achievement*, documents that it's not the income of the home or the number of parents in the home, but the quality of the interaction. Those parents who instill in their children high expectations, believe they, the parents, are the primary educators, and are consistent and complementary in their discipline produce excellent students.

Sonya Carson, the mother of Dr. Ben Carson, the famous pediatric neurosurgeon, was able to achieve excellent results with her sons simply by adjusting two variables. She reduced television viewing and increased reading time. I strongly encourage all parents to increase reading and consider either no television during the week or a maximum of one hour per day. The least we can do is equalize reading time and television viewing.

In my book *Countering the Conspiracy to Destroy Black Boys*, we observed parents who, in spite of the conspiracy, were able to produce excellent results in their sons. Two of the steps that mothers and fathers took, primarily mothers, were to monitor their children's peer group and limit the amount of time they spent on the street. They understood the

# Family and Health

distinction between playing alley ball and structured sports. The latter provides their kids with a coach, discipline, and a structured regimen that all children need.

Many single mothers who have successfully raised their sons utilized the extended family. While the biological father was not present, they enlisted their brother, uncle, grandfather, co-worker, or neighbor to act as a positive role model and spend time with their sons. Many of these single mothers also utilized the church, rites of passage, Saturday academies, martial arts programs, etc.

I have worked with youth for over three decades. I can almost predict who will be successful by observing three areas:

1. Attitude
2. Respect for authority
3. Chores

Many of our youth have a bad attitude and carry a chip on their shoulder. It does not require much provocation for them to fight and swear. Youth workers must use scriptures and motivational stories to improve their attitude.

Many parents have only required their children to respect them and not the larger village. Unfortunately, some parents have not even mandated that their children respect them. The million-dollar challenge is how to teach children whose parents have been negligent to accept authority. It requires committed adults who understand this to be a vital part of the equation that must be addressed. Many athletic coaches have risen to the challenge and have done a fantastic job of filling the authority void in young lives.

The last variable is chores. Many youth are irresponsible because they were never given meaningful tasks to accomplish. My good friend, Alicia Jackson at MEE Productions in

Philadelphia, has conducted informal surveys of her staff over the years, and she has concluded that the lack of chores in their early lives explains their tardiness, absenteeism, lack of cleanliness, poor work ethic, poor quality work, and overall lack of professionalism. How can youth become responsible if parents do not give them chores?

**Health**
African Americans have the greatest incidence of disease or involvement in all of the following conditions:
Heart disease
Diabetes
High blood pressure
Stroke
Kidney failure
Fibroid tumors
AIDS
Obesity
Low life expectancy
Infertility
Infant death
Lung cancer
Prostate cancer
Pancreatic cancer
Liver cancer

There's a tremendous difference in the incidence of stroke in White women living in the state of Minnesota and Black males living in Mississippi. The latter is a soul food mecca and part of the stroke belt. What are the four major ingredients of soul food? Pork, grease, salt, and sugar. If we're going to reduce the incidence of disease, we must reduce if not eliminate pork, fried food, salt, and sugar from our diet. Furthermore, we must pay greater attention to our health. Minnesota has one of the largest aggregations of health food stores, colon therapists, and exercise clubs in the country.

What health success models do we have in the African American community? The Seventh Day Adventists are a Christian denomination that believes in a vegetarian diet. They have the least incidence of heart disease, cancer, and high blood pressure. It's not an accident. Their health is directly related to their diet, which is not a soul food diet. Muslims also have less incidence of high blood pressure and heart disease because they do not eat pork. There is also less incidence of lung cancer and cirrhosis of the liver among people who do not smoke or drink excessively.

We'll talk about Salem in the chapter on "The Black Church," but their Pastor, James Meeks in Chicago, Illinois, has been successful at ridding their community of all liquor stores. In the typical Black community, you will find plenty of barbecue shops, funeral homes, liquor stores and gas stations on the four corners. We can reduce disease by reducing the number of liquor stores and barbecue joints. Where in the Black community can you find a juice bar, salad bar, colon therapist, or health food grocery? This lack reflects death in our community. How can a people be faulted if healthful institutions, services, and products don't exist for them?

In my book *Satan, I'm Taking Back My Health!,* I speak of three essential measures that we must all take. Our bodies consist of 80 percent water. It is absolutely necessary that we increase our water consumption, ideally to eight glasses per day. Second, we must realize that we come from the earth. Our bodies reflect the earth. We are made of 103 minerals, nutrients, and vitamins. It is our daily responsibility to eat those foods that contain those 103 minerals, nutrients, and vitamins. Unfortunately, the soil now has very little of the nutrients and vitamins and minerals that our parents consumed in the early 1900s. It is going to require a greater effort to consume the foods necessary for good health. Lastly, we all need to exercise enough to burn off the excess calories that we consume.

I wanted this chapter on "Family and Health" to precede the next chapter on "Economics", because wealth is not just measured in financial terms; it is also evaluated based on health and marital stability. In the book *The Millionaire Next Door*, almost all of the millionaires stayed married to one person. Divorce is destructive and costly. Child support payments can become very expensive. Unfortunately, many of us have been unable to build a strong economic base because 25 to 50 percent of our paycheck goes for alimony and child support payments. In addition, many of us haven't been able to develop ourselves economically because of poor health.

Many people have told me that they would love to become entrepreneurs, but they cannot leave their job because it provides medical benefits. It's a sad commentary that workers are not able to become employers due to health considerations. It is even more tragic when people like Reggie Lewis, the great businessman who acquired Beatrice Foods for $985 million, was unable to see his 50th birthday.

The Bible reminds us in 3 John: 2, "Beloved, I pray that you prosper in all things and be in health just as your soul prospers." Prosperity is not limited to financial wealth. It includes health, good family life, and a personal relationship with a Savior who will never leave you or forsake you.

In the next chapter, "Economics," we will offer strategies to improve the current four-corner Black community.

# CHAPTER 6

 CONOMICS

I want to charge you with the responsibility of being president of Black America. So many times people ask, "What are Jesse Jackson Sr., Louis Farrakhan, Al Sharpton, Kweisi Mfume, and numerous others doing?"

As president of Black America, the following are your assets:

$688 billion collective income
900,000 businesses
$80 billion in business receipts
4 million college graduates
2 million college students
102+ Black colleges
38 banks
200+ radio stations
200+ newspapers
85,000 churches who receive $3 billion annually and possess $50 billion in assets[13]

The major problem is that because we do not see ourselves as a nation, we only spend 4 percent of our $688 billion with our 900,000 businesses. It has been said that we would have to return to the Jim Crow era to increase that percentage. Is that true? Yet every billion dollars African Americans spend with Black businesses produces 50,000 jobs.

With the loss of three million manufacturing jobs, every effort must be made to create adequate paying jobs. This should be the number one agenda item for every African American leader and politician. For African American pastors, after bringing people to Christ, this should be their number two priority. For the four million African Americans with degrees, and all those with a skill, we must ask ourselves, how many people do we employ? Parents must encourage their children to become entrepreneurs. We must leverage our 24 million eligible votes to demand from the government, job creation in the African American community.

In Chapter 8, we will look at the phenomenon of lack of unity and support from an historical and psychological perspective; but in many ways, this chapter on economics is the most important chapter in the book. What good is it to earn $688 billion if African Americans cheat themselves by spending only 4 percent of it with each other? Obviously, it is difficult to separate economics from Africentricity.

There are numerous studies that like to compare immigrants to slaves. Many of the Black conservatives like comparing the relative success of Jews and African Americans, Asians and African Americans, Hispanics and African Americans, Arabs and African Americans. There's even research comparing Africans from the continent of Africa or the Caribbean with African Americans. In those comparisons, immigrants surpass African Americans in almost every economic and educational indicator. Average sales per firm:

| | |
|---|---|
| Asians | $336,000 |
| Hispanics | $155,000 |
| African Americans | $86,000 |

In terms of annual average family income:

| | |
|---|---|
| Asians | $55,000 |
| Whites | $46,000 |
| Hispanics | $33,000 |
| African Americans | $30,000 |

# Economics

Business started per 1,000 persons:

| | |
|---|---|
| Arabs | 108 |
| Asians | 96 |
| Whites | 64 |
| Hispanics | 19 |
| African Americans | 9[14] |

You cannot give 96 percent of your income away and blame 100 percent of your problems on someone else. It's no accident that only nine African Americans per thousand start a business, when most of them are aware that because of self-hatred and lack of cultural appreciation, only 4 percent of African Americans dollars will come to their African American business.

First, every African American must review their checkbook to determine how much they are spending with African American businesses. Put an "A" next to the African American business and put an "F" next to the non-African American business. Set a goal that you will spend 20 percent of your income with African American businesses. Notice, I did not say 100 percent, because I'm aware that it would be impossible to spend your entire income with African American businesses: we do not manufacture cars, provide utilities, refine gasoline, etc. Realistically, we should shoot for 20 percent as our goal.

Let's revisit the immigrant model. It is unfair to compare someone who voluntarily came here with their culture intact, to a people who were forced to come here and took their culture from slave owners. In the Africentricity chapter, we will discuss this in more detail, but for now, there's much that we can learn from the immigrant model.

Let's first look at the Jewish community. How many Jews do you know on welfare? The average American only gives 2 percent of their disposable income to charity compared to 4 percent for Jews. The annual campaign for the United Jewish Appeal collects about $1 billion annually, drawing from 2.5 percent of the total U.S. population. The United Way annual campaign, in contrast, attracts 32 million contributors (11 percent of the population) and raises $3.6 billion.

With the possible exception of the Salvation Army, the United Jewish Appeal raises more money per contributor than any individual charity in America, including the American Red Cross, Catholic Charities, and the American Cancer Society. The Jewish Federation is the organization that coordinates financial planning, and leadership activities among existing Jewish organizations in an area. These federations exist in every city of any consequence in the United States. They were conceived and founded in order to interconnect members of the Jewish Diaspora who arrived in America from many different nations, speaking many different languages, but still needing to relate to one another, defend one another, and assure progress socially, politically, educationally, and culturally.

The issues addressed by the Jewish federations include identity, family values, education, scholarships, and social justice. The Jewish Federation consists of local organizations. Local groups perceived a need to create an umbrella organization to represent all of the federations. The Council of Jewish Federations in North America was founded in 1932 to meet that need. The general assembly of the council brings together more than 3,000 Jewish leaders annually to consider new ideas, distribute materials, and share experiences.[15]

The Jewish community, which only has 2.5 percent of the U.S. population, has 11 percent of the U. S. Senators and dominates the legal, banking, and media industries. It has always been amazing to me that people say the Black

# Economics

community is poor and that it's difficult for businesses to profit in this community. Yet Jews, Asians, Arabs, and others do very well in the Black community. The following quote from Claud Anderson in his book *Powernomics* best describes the economic problem in the Black community.

> A Black marketing organization approached a group of Asian merchants in an effort to sell them a variety of popular consumer items. After the Black distributors made their sales pitch, they were disappointed when the Asian merchant replied that they were not interested in purchasing products the Black distributors were selling. Determined not to give up on the Asian merchants, the Black distributors offered a 25 percent discount from the price that the Asian merchants would pay for the same items. Again, the Asians told the Black distributors they were not interested. In a collective voice of puzzlement, the Black distributors asked how the merchants could afford to turn down a 25 percent discount. The merchants responded, "You Black people just don't understand. It is not the money but the fact that we only buy from our own. Only you Blacks will buy from any and everyone."[16]

Two of the models that I want to recommend are Matah and Ujamaa. Matah was founded in 1997 and is a national organization with great potential. It has done reasonably well with its limited financial resources. The leadership of Matah has assembled more than 300 products, ranging from toiletries and appliances to clothing, books, etc. The objective is for African American businesses to expand and sell the Matah product line. A second objective is for African American consumers to seek out Matah products. Thus far, the movement has been grassroots. It is difficult for Matah to pay $40,000 for a full-page ad in Ebony or Essence. I encourage all readers to go to the Matah website, become more familiar with their products, and identify vendors in your local area that sell Matah items.

The second model is Ujamaa. I have learned from Arabs, Asians, and other immigrants that they do not start their businesses with loans from banks. Because they value their history and culture and realize the importance of unity, they pool their resources to start their businesses. The Ujamaa model requires the following:

1. Everyone comes to the meeting with a business plan.
2. Everyone brings $100 to the meeting.
3. Participants agree that whomever has the best plan will receive all the money.
4. Whoever has the best plan agrees that they will support the other businesses present.
5. Members return the following week or month and repeat the process until everyone who desires start-up capital will have the necessary funds.

How do the White man, racism, and White supremacy circumvent our ability to implement Ujamaa? I encourage you to create an Ujamaa meeting so that we can increase the number of African American businesses.

Another factor that contributes to the lack of economic development in the Black community is parenting. Unfortunately, there are too many African American parents that instill in their children the desire to secure a good job while immigrant parents teach their children to secure a good business. There is also different schooling for future employees and employers. Many African American students attend

# Economics

schools where teachers view them as future employees, if not inmates. They lower expectations and alter their pedagogy.

If you want to develop an employee, you discourage the student from asking questions, and you only ask questions when the answer is predetermined. Employees should never know more than their employers, and students should never know more than their teachers. If you only ask what you already know, the best scenario is that your students will know what you know and nothing more.

In schooling for future employers, teachers encourage students to ask the majority of the questions, and teachers ask open-ended questions. Children are now learning via discovery, which is another reason why schools still believe in tracking. When schools divide students into advanced placement, honors, gifted, talented, regular, remedial, and special education, what they have done is to create schools for employers and schools for employees.

I'd like to present four organizations that offer economic solutions for parents and schools. First, let me recommend the National Foundation for Teaching Entrepreneurship. This organization, of which I'm an advisory board member, has been in existence for almost 20 years. They have created excellent curriculum materials to teach youth entrepreneurship. In addition, they train staff nationwide to work with school districts, community organizations, and churches.

The second organization is Black Enterprise, with their Teenpreneur and Kidpreneur programs. They hold a national conference, where children's business plans are displayed, evaluated, and rewarded. There has been a great response and many kids have gone on to develop businesses. Third, I recommend Operation Hope founded by John Bryant. Their program, Banking on Our Future, has taught thousands of youth economic literacy. A similar program is the Development School for Youth founded by Dr. Lenora Fulani.

Last, I encourage every church and organization to provide Wealth Empowerment Seminars. Black Enterprise has distributed over 100,000 Wealth Building Kits. One of the major problems in the African American community is that many of us do not understand the distinction between income and wealth. Listed below are some of the areas that need to be taught in the seminars.

1. Pay God first (tithe 10 percent of your gross income). Only 26 percent of Christians are tithers.
2. Pay yourself second (10 percent).
3. Develop a budget.
4. Understand the distinction between needs and wants, income and wealth.
5. Buy a moderately priced car, drive it for a long time, and save thousands.
6. Brown bag a lunch once a week and save thousands.
7. Use $5 worth of grocery coupons a week and save thousands.
8. Eat at home more frequently and save thousands.
9. Skip daily junk food and expensive coffees at work and save thousands.
10. Smoking is hazardous to your wealth. Quit and save thousands.
11. Buy term insurance and invest the difference of thousands.
12. Before investing, learn Rule 72 (72 divided by the interest rate will determine the number of years it will take to double your money).

# Economics

13. Secure a 15-year mortgage, or accelerate your 30-year payments.
14. Unless you pay cash for everything, understand that your credit worthiness is your key to success. Monitor your credit report.
15. Always pay your bills on time.
16. Pay the maximum amount on your credit cards; ideally pay the entire balance monthly.
17. Buy assets that appreciate, such as stocks, bonds, and real estate. Avoid assets that depreciate, such as cars, clothes, and jewelry. Only 46 percent of African Americans are homeowners in contrast to 72 percent of Whites. The car note should never exceed the rent payment. Houses should be bought before cars. Ironically, the mortgage is almost the same as the rent payment. The challenge is the down payment and repairing your credit. The football star Warrick Dunn has created Home for the Holidays. He provides single mothers with the home down payment, furnishings, and money management and home maintenance classes. We need more athletes like Dunn.

I respect Jesse Jackson Sr. and the Wall Street Project. They realize that African Americans should be at the table when decisions are made about where pension and mutual funds should be invested. In addition, as stockholders, African Americans should attend corporate meetings to avoid future Enron fiascos. When cities are involved in bond development, African Americans should be involved in the financing.

I encourage everyone to read Booker T. Washington, Marcus Garvey, and Elijah Muhammad. Unfortunately, many

African Americans refer to Booker T. Washington as a Tom, and yet it was Washington who invited Marcus Garvey to come to America. Washington, Garvey, and Muhammad developed economic models that need to be studied, improved, and replicated. Washington's blue-collar philosophy could keep our youth from selling drugs. Garvey and Muhammad's philosophy "do for self" and entrepreneurship could eliminate our unemployment rate of 12 percent.

It disappoints me that there are African Americans with bachelor's, master's, and PhD degrees who are unemployed. As much as I value white-collar skills, I believe one way to measure education is by securing a balance between blue- and white-collar skills.

Another solution comes from the great work of Rev. Charles Koen. He is the founder and director of the United Front. He has created carpenter's training schools in Chicago and East St. Louis, Illinois. He is training numerous males and females for blue-collar trades. He's creating for them the opportunity to develop much needed housing throughout the state. After integration in 1954, we belittled blue-collar skills.

The Bible teaches us that all work is honorable unto the Lord, and if a man does not work, he does not eat. Something is wrong when there are construction projects in the Black community, with outsiders dong all the work while brothers hang on corners wasting their time away. Are Hispanics the only group willing to landscape, clean houses, hotels, and offices, and wash dishes?

The late Maynard Jackson told the city of Atlanta that "if you think we're going to build this airport without Black labor, you are sadly mistaken." He promised he would shut construction down. Power brokers understood and respected

# Economics

Maynard Jackson. The airport was built with more than 30 percent participation from the African American community.

Another solution is Kazi. This is the Swahili word for work. Wealth is far more than dollars. It's human capital. It's the four million African Americans who have degrees and the two million who are pursuing college. Beyond that, human capital is reflected in the large numbers of "disconnected" African American men and women who wake up every morning with energy, a brain, but unfortunately are unemployed. In a capitalistic society, many of us have allowed ourselves to be reduced to a dollar bill. If you understand that you, as an individual, represent wealth, then you realize that you have human capital.

The Kazi solution is recommended for every community organization and church. You will need a good administrator and computer. The program operates as follows:

1.  The unemployed worker signs up with Kazi to barter their labor.
2.  The administrator sends the Kazi worker to perform X number of hours of work for a client.
3.  The worker's account is credited with the hours worked.
4.  The worker then contacts the Kazi coordinator to receive those hours in services from another worker.

The essence of the Kazi program is bartering and exchanging labor without the dollar bill as the medium of exchange.

Another solution involves the largest 150 Black organizations, which includes the Urban League, NAACP, Operation PUSH, fraternities, sororities, churches, etc. These organizations spend $16 billion annually. At most of their annual conferences they talk about the plight and dilemmas of the Black community. Many of the organizations blame the White man for their problems. The reality is that while blaming the White man, they spend $16 billion with Misters Hilton, Hyatt, and Marriott, not to mention United, American, and Delta Airlines. I'm sure these hotels and airlines are encouraging these 150 organizations to talk about them all the way to the bank.

What would happen if these Black organizations chose not to meet for one year, saved the $16 billion, and in the following year built four regional hotels called Ramses Palace, Marcus Garvey Suites, Harriet Tubman Villas, and Rosa Park Resorts, along with obtaining a fleet of corporate jets? Romans 4:17 says, "Call those things that do not exist as though they were."

I understand some of the difficulties with this solution. For many organizations, their national conference is their major fundraiser. Without this conference they would not have the monies needed to finance their operation. If we were better stewards of our budgets, we could create more of a surplus. Another criticism has been that they've already signed contracts with Misters Hilton, Hyatt, or Marriott, and the financial penalties would be exorbitant. My suggestion would be to appeal the contract and if to no avail, honor the contract and avoid future commitments. A third challenge to this solution questions our assumption that the Baptists, Omegas, and NAACP members would send their money to the national office even though they did not attend the conference; we hope they would.

In the meantime, while we are waiting for these organizations we can meet at HBCUs and churches. We need to support the Royal Palm Crowne Plaza in Miami Beach. It is the first Black developed and owned luxury resort in the

# Economics

nation. This hotel is a result of a 1,000-day boycott that cost the Miami tourism industry $52 million, because of their disrespect of Nelson Mandela's visit in 1993. In the last chapter on "Implementation," we will discuss these issues in more detail.

Another solution that does not require as much of a sacrifice involves $1. There are approximately 36 million African Americans in the United States. If we announce today that we want each one to contribute $1, and even the homeless have $1, we would possess $36 million. We have the numbers, and all of us have $1. That is not the problem. The challenge is who would we trust to hold $36 million? That's why it's difficult to discuss economics without looking at Africentricity and the importance of culture and unity. You could have the greatest economic ideas, but without unity, without Africentricity, without an understanding of the Nguzo Saba and Ma'at, these great economic ideas would not be implemented.

The reality is that many immigrants and other groups not only understand economics, but they also understand the importance of history and culture. Maybe our people would trust a board that included Oprah Winfrey, Bill Cosby, and Robert Johnson, since they are already billionaires and have demonstrated a track record of good financial stewardship.

Another solution—vertical integration (the control of land, raw materials, manufacturing, distributing, and retailing)—comes from my good friend and author, Claud Anderson.

Other ethnic and racial groups have looked at the entire economy and have created niches for themselves. They assess their strengths. Earlier, I mentioned that the Jewish community specializes in law, finance, and media. The Asian community specializes in the laundry and food industries. The Hispanic community has specialized in landscaping and the food and services industries. The Arab community specializes in the retail industry.

What industries do African Americans control? What industries lend themselves as opportunities for African Americans? In what industries are we large consumers or do we have major expertise?

Some of the industries are hair care, clothing, music, sports, and soul food. Those are industries where African Americans should dominate. Because we have such an obsession with "good hair" (not believing that God gave us good hair) and the need to turn those beautiful curls straight, we are the only consumer in this market. How can African Americans be the only consumer in a market and yet have only a 30 percent market share? We had a greater market share 30 years ago.

The American Health and Beauty Aids Institute (AHBAI) represents Black hair care companies. Their primary objective is to influence African American consumers to support their own. An African queen is placed as a symbol on their products to inform the consumer that the item came from a Black-owned company. Many White-owned companies like Revlon use Black movie stars like Halle Berry to entice Black consumers. Today AHBAI is struggling with less than 10 members. The surviving members owe their success to AHBAI and the Salon Advantage Club. Foreign merchants underpriced Black retailers and made other hair care products manufactured by White firms available to consumers. Black hair care manufacturers, however, have garnered great support from Black hair care salons. These products are only available through stylists. We must invigorate this organization. We can't lose any more Soft Sheens and Johnson Products.

# Economics

Can you imagine the NBA without African Americans? Eighty-four percent of the NBA are African Americans. I commend Robert Johnson who owns the Charlotte team. Michael Jordan, Isaiah Thomas, and Magic Johnson are just a few who also have similar ownership desires.

I also commend Johnnie Cochran and the other lawyers who were involved in putting pressure on the NFL to increase Black ownership and coaches in the league. The NFL is far more than players. The sports industry is a trillion-dollar operation that includes ownership, stadiums, vendors, promotions, agents, etc. Can you imagine an NFL or NBA team with an all White lineup? Yet, over 90 percent of the agents, receptionists, janitors, vendors, and all other ancillary businesses are White. We need African American ballplayers to demand more than an increase in salary.

Another industry that relies on Black people is music. Can you imagine the music industry without African American participation? On October 4, 2003, African American artists occupied all of the 10 spots on the Billboard bestseller list. The real money in the music industry is not with the artists. P. Diddy and Russell Simmons understand that. It's in production and distribution. Let me present the following scenario.

A rapper sells 1 million CDs:
1. The CD sells for $18.
2. The distributor receives 50 percent of all sales. ($9 million)
3. The producer receives 45 percent of all sales. ($8.1 million)
4. The rapper receives 5 percent of all sales. ($900,000)
5. The rapper is responsible for all studio and video production costs. ($500,000).
6. There are four rappers who receive a paltry $100,000.

We need more control over this industry. I respect underground rappers who sell one million CDs and cut out the distributor.

Another Black-reliant industry is clothing. Of the $688 billion that we earn, we spend almost $30 billion on clothing. It is not an accident that African American secretaries outdress their bosses, and African Americans in ghettos drive better cars than affluent Whites who live in suburbs. Clothing is a major industry that we need to control. We need to support Karl Kani, F.U.B.U. (For Us By Us), P. Diddy's Sean John line, among others. We must be careful because the clothing industry is similar to the hair care industry. Many companies that appear to be Black owned are actually owned by non-African Americans.

The last industry I'll mention is soul food. If Asians were the only ones who bought Chinese and Thai food, they would not be selling it in the quantities we witness. Asians not only like their own food, but they have exported their cuisine to other communities; they understand that their income should also come from the larger population. We need to export soul food, perhaps modified for better nutrition, to other communities for economic (not to mention taste) reasons. African Americans should not be the only consumers of soul food.

The idea behind vertical integration is to control the entire industry, from manufacturing and distribution to retailing. In 1910, African Americans owned 16 million acres of land and there were 926,000 Black farmers. Presently, we own less than 2 million acres of land and there are only 18,000 farmers. We need to support Muhammad Farms, owned by the Nation of Islam in Georgia, the Republic of New Africa, which owns

# Economics

land in Mississippi, and the Shrine of the Black Madonna, which owns Beulah Land in South Carolina.

The NAACP facilitated an agreement between Black farmers and Cuba. The latter has agreed to buy a percentage of its produce from Black farmers. The National Coalition of Minority Growers and Agribusiness attempts to coordinate its Black farmers with major supermarkets. In addition, they help their farmers sell produce in Black communities. Can you imagine the benefits of coordinating Black farmers and the soul food industry? Glory Foods is a shining example, and they illustrate the potential that exists for a coalition of farmers, distributors, supermarkets, and consumers.

Another solution is reparations. One of the major reasons, why it's unfair to compare immigrants to enslaved Africans, is because the latter were denied wages for their labor and were unable to own property or to secure an education. What is the financial cost for free labor between 1619 and 1865 plus interest and penalty? Some estimate $10 trillion. There is some old money in America. One percent of the population owns 48 percent of the wealth. Ten percent of the population owns 86 percent of the wealth. You would have to be stupid not to earn a profit if people work for you for free for 246 years.

The following chart will give you an idea of the labor cost of plantation owners during slavery.

| Year | Average price of an enslaved African |
|------|--------------------------------------|
| 1800 | $600 |
| 1810 | $900 |
| 1820 | $1050 |
| 1840 | $1200 |
| 1860 | $1600 |
| 1862 | $1800[17] |

Representative John Conyers of Detroit for more than two decades has tried to introduce legislation into Congress on the issue of reparations. His initial desire is simply for Congress to discuss reparations, and investigate the impact slavery has had on the African American community.

What are the historical precedents for reparations? What did America do for Asians who were placed in concentration camps for two to six years during World War II?

How did America compensate Native Americans for taking much of their land? The following table provides answers.

### EXAMPLES OF REPARATIONS PAYMENTS

| | | |
|---|---|---|
| 1952 Germany | $822 million | Holocaust Survivors |
| 1971 United States | $1 billion + 44 million acres of land | Alaska Natives Land Settlement |
| 1980 United States | $81 million | Klamaths of Oregon |
| 1985 United States | $105 million | Lakota of South Dakota |
| 1985 United States | $12.3 million | Seminoles of Florida |
| 1985 United States | $31 million | Chippewas of Wisconsin |
| 1986 United States | $32 million for 1836 treaty violations | Ottawas of Michigan |
| 1988 Canada | $230 million | Japanese Canadians |
| 1988 Canada | 250,000 square miles of land | Eskimos and Indigenous People |
| 1990 Austria | $25 million | Jewish Claims on Austria |
| 1990 United States | $1.2 billion | Japanese Americans[18] |

Frederick Douglass reminded us that power concedes nothing without a struggle. Under the leadership of N'COBRA, the Black United Front, and the Republic of New Africa, there is a tremendous movement afloat to push for reparations. The

# Economics

objective is not for 36 million African Americans to individually receive X number of dollars. The objectives are as follows:
1.   Publicize the cost.
2.   Apologize.
3.   Restitution.

They recommend that reparations be used to create law schools, medical schools, television networks, additional colleges, radio stations, national newspapers, hospitals, scholarships, housing, business grants, and land acquisition.

More than 30 years ago, the Urban League recommended a "Marshal Plan" to rebuild the Black community after the rebellions of the 1960s. How unfortunate that we can find billions of dollars to rebuild Iraq, but we can't find millions of dollars to build the Black community.

I strongly recommend that the government revisit the Marshal Plan. America has rebuilt Germany, is now rebuilding Iraq, but continues to ignore the Black community.

In the next chapter on "Politics and Organizing," we will look at the relationship between economics and politics. Let me close this chapter with the following table, describing the relationship between economics and politics.

# SOLUTIONS FOR BLACK AMERICA

| Year | Number of Black Elected Officials | % of Blacks Unemployed | % of Blacks in Prison | % of Blacks Below the Poverty Line | Black per Capita Income to Whites |
|---|---|---|---|---|---|
| 1964 | 103 | 10 | 33 | 34 | 53 |
| 1970 | 1439 | 8 | 36 | 33 | 60 |
| 1975 | 3503 | 15 | 42 | 31 | 55 |
| 1988 | 6793 | 12 | 45 | 32 | 60 |
| 1992 | 8000 | 15 | 45 | 34 | 59[19] |
| 2004 | 9000 + | 14 | 52 | 33 | 60 |

# CHAPTER 7

# POLITICS AND ORGANIZING

Politics is the distribution system for economics. It determines who gets what, when, where, why, how much, and for how long. The late, great former mayor of Atlanta, Maynard Jackson, from a political standpoint was able to dictate that the Atlanta airport would not be built without one-third of the contractors being African American. He produced several millionaires.

Many cities have developed set asides and affirmative action programs, that allow African Americans and other groups to receive a certain percentage of all city contracts. When a White contractor, Croson, protested affirmative action in Richmond, Virginia, and the court decided in his favor, there followed a 70 percent drop off in city contracts to African Americans.

Every time I drive by a construction site in the inner city, I'm looking for the number and percentage of African American workers on the site. It is an insult and a slap in our face for a city to be 50 percent or more African American and have literally no African Americans on public work sites.

I strongly recommend that we develop in every city an organization that will monitor employment activities. If we do not have adequate representation on those construction sites, then we must march and protest, shut the city down until we receive our fair share.

I also recommend that we determine the percentage of African American students in our public schools in every city, attend school board meetings, and challenge the board to award the same percentage of school contracts as there are Black students to African American firms. In most cities, not only are African American children being miseducated, but their parents receive back in the form of paychecks very little of the school budget.

In addition, politics determines the available pool of jurors for a court case. If African Americans are not registered to vote, they are ineligible to be jurors. This becomes very significant when more than 50 percent of America's inmates are African American. In order to better appreciate this chapter, listed below are the numbers that drive our political destiny.

203 million eligible U.S. voters
130 million registered U.S. voters
105 million voted in the 2000 presidential election
24 million eligible African American voters
16 million registered African American voters
12 million African Americans voted in the 2000 election
92 percent voted Democratic
8 percent voted Republican
1.5 million are ineligible to vote because of felonies.

9,000 + elected officials
621 federal and state
5,420 city and county
1,922 education related
1, 037 law enforcement

States with the highest elected officials
Mississippi        897
Alabama            731
Louisiana          701

# Politics and Organizing

In the chart on the last page of the previous chapter, you noticed that an increase in elected officials did not reduce unemployment, prison inmates, or poverty. There are myriad factors involved, but in this chapter on politics we need to honestly ask ourselves, "Have some politicians stayed too long?" Do they have the same vigor as in their first years? Is a political office a lifelong position? I respect former Congressmen Floyd Flake, Kweisi Mfume, and William Gray who walked away from $100,000 + salaries and expenses and found other careers. Would term limits benefit the Black community? I think so. It is very difficult to defeat an incumbent, Black or White, without term limits.

The fundamental challenge for African Americans is how to leverage 24 million eligible votes into a proportionate amount of political power? If African Americans constitute 12 percent of the population, ideally we should have 6 governors, 12 senators, and 52 congresspersons. The reality is that we have no governors or senators and only 39 congresspersons. In the states of Mississippi, Alabama, and Louisiana, we represent almost one-third of the voters, but have few elected officials. The problem has been that African Americans will vote for White candidates, but seldom will White candidates vote for African Americans.

Malcolm X called many southern White Democrats "Dixiecrats", because many of them left the Democratic Party due to the large percentage of African Americans in southern states who were voting Democratic. In South Carolina, in the 2000 gubernatorial election, the Democrat lost by 40,000 votes, but there were 400,000 African Americans unregistered. In Georgia in 2000, the Democratic senator lost by 30,000 votes; there were 600,000 African Americans unregistered.

If we are going to effectively use our political power, we cannot work with half our ammunition. We have 24 million eligible voters, but only 12 million vote. It is difficult to win a sports activity when only half your team is playing.

I commend every state legislator like Connie Howard of Illinois and numerous others across the country who have written legislation that would expunge the record and restore voting privileges to former inmates. In the presidential election of 2000, Al Gore received 50,992,000 votes. George W. Bush received 50,455,000 votes. The election easily could have been decided just by the 1.5 million African Americans who were denied the right to vote because of a past felony. It is a contradiction for America to promote democracy in Iraq and other parts of the world, yet deny its own citizens the right to vote. I encourage every African American to write their legislators to advocate expungement. I commend Jesse Jackson, Sr., and the Rainbow-PUSH Coalition, NAACP, SCLC, Urban League, National Coalition for Black Voter Participation, and the Hip Hop Summit, spearheaded by Russell Simmons and Ben Chavis, for increasing registration and voting.

Historically, what have African Americans received for their 92 percent loyalty to the Democratic Party? In the 2000 presidential election and Florida debacle, you would have thought that this was a Black-White issue. African Americans were fighting for their right to be represented in Florida, and the Democratic Party literally had them defend themselves. Al Sharpton made a profound statement:

> The Democratic Party acts like we are their mistress that they have to hide, like we're some political scarlet whore rather than their respected partner. Either we're going to have a healthy marriage or we're getting a divorce and marrying someone who will respect us. We will no longer allow ourselves to be screwed by the Democrats.[20]

# Politics and Organizing

The above quote drives this chapter and raises the question, What have we received for our 92 percent voting loyalty? Many African Americans who have become disenchanted with the lack of respect, appreciation, and agenda importance from the Democratic Party have moved elsewhere. Recent polls from the Joint Center for Political and Economic Studies indicate that 27 percent of African Americans view themselves as Independents. Ten percent view themselves as Republicans. This trend is even more pronounced in the age group 26 to 35, where an increasing number of African Americans are choosing to become Independents and Republicans.

What did we get in 1988 when Jesse Jackson, Sr., received six million votes in the Democratic primaries alone? In the 2004 presidential primaries, one of the major challenges that Al Sharpton and Carol Mosley Braun faced was finances. George W. Bush had $100 million to run his campaign. Many Democratic leaders have $20 to $40 million. Al Sharpton and Carol Mosley Braun were trying to run their presidential campaigns with less than $500,000, each.

Do you need $40 million to run for the presidency? Do you need $10 million to run for governor or senator and $5 million for mayor? Could the major reason why 12 million African Americans are either unregistered or choose not to vote, be attributed to the fact that they don't like voting for the lesser of two rich evils? Let me quickly mention that while I don't advocate voting for the lesser of two evils as the major reason for voting, it is still important to vote: in 2000 Bill Clinton left office with a record $150 billion surplus; by 2004, George Bush had created a $512 billion deficit.

It was announced that we won the war in Iraq, but every day after the war supposedly ended, American soldiers were killed. Do you think things would have been different if Gore had been president? Do you think the deficit would have been less? Do you think that dealing with Iraq would have been less expensive? Why did we use military force with Iraq and not with North Korea, if they both supposedly had nuclear arms and weapons of mass destruction? Was this a war about oil?

Let's return to the original question:

What do African Americans want in return for their 24 million potential votes?

1. We demand our fair share of governmental contracts.
2. We demand inmates' records be expunged.
3. Reparations must be considered in Congress.
4. Inmates must receive rehabilitation and drug treatment.
5. Head Start, Title I, Leave No Child Behind, and Pell Grants should be adequately funded.
6. Racial profiling and police brutality must be eliminated.
7. Unemployment must be reduced.
8. Job training must be increased.
9. Health care must be provided.

I strongly recommend that we review and study the re-creation of an independent Black political party. In 1980 in Philadelphia, we created the National Black Independent Political Party (NBIPP). We need to study our history, especially the conferences that we had in Gary, Little Rock, and Philadelphia. I encourage everyone to join the National Black United Front and familiarize themselves with Ron Daniels and the Center for Constitutional Rights.

# Politics and Organizing

The second part of this chapter is about organizing, which is a major component of politics. I strongly encourage you to read Oba T'Shaka and his powerful book *The Art of Leadership*. If we are going to effectively organize 36 million African Americans, 24 million of whom are eligible to vote, we must master the principles of organizing.

Kwame Nkrumah offered these words of advice: "Go to the people. Live among them. Learn from them. Love them. Plan with them. Start with what they know. Build on what they have."[21]

We can also learn from Amil Cabral. He was a brilliant organizer and leader of the revolution in Guinea Bissau. He internalized the principles of Nkrumah. Cabral, like the Honorable Elijah Muhammad, understood that only intellectuals argue over ideas. The masses of people are concerned with basic goods and services. At the outset of this book, I mentioned that my heart is with the 20 percent of our race that is living below the poverty line, 50 percent of whom are children, and the one million that earn less than $7,000 annually. Who has the agenda for them?

The Black middle and upper class argue about socialism, capitalism, communism, or whether we're going to say "Africentricity" or "Africentricity." Cabral and Muhammad understood that the masses of people are not concerned about those issues. They're concerned about survival and basic goods and services.

We need to study how the Nation of Islam under the leadership of the late Honorable Elijah Muhammad, without the $28,000 that states spend per inmate, notwithstanding a recidivism rate of 85 percent, converted Detroit Red to Malcolm X. I'll never forget how the Honorable Louis Farrakhan on the Donahue Show challenged White America when he said, "Why don't you give us the inmates? It would save you money. You don't know what to do with them, and we do." If America was trying to balance the budget, they should have agreed to Farrakhan's offer. Obviously, balancing the budget is not a major objective of American politicians. They are very much aware that prisons are ineffective. Head Start, Title I, and Pell Grants, however, are highly effective.

Muhammad converted Detroit Red to Malcolm X with spirituality, Africentricity, entrepreneurship, nutrition, and discipline. When I was in college in Illinois State, I founded an organization called Unity. Implementing the theories of Cabral, Muhammad, and Nkrumah, I studied my peers and observed their needs. The university did not provide a Sunday dinner, so we had a rally and a forum every Sunday evening. If you attended the rally, you were entitled to receive dinner from Unity. Many students were in dire need of tutorial services. If they became a member of Unity, we provided tutoring for them.

Unfortunately, most people join organizations for selfish reasons. Cabral and Muhammad understood that. People join organizations with the hidden agenda, "What's in it for me?" I have often wondered how, before the weekend induction process when hazing was rampant, a person could pledge Omega Psi Phi fraternity and upon completion of going over the "golden sands," would be branded and say, "I'll be a Q to the day I die." What happened during that eight- to twelve-week pledging process that motivated a person to be branded with the Omega Symbol on their body?

How many Christians have that level of commitment to our Lord and Savior Jesus Christ? Do we have that level of commitment to Operation PUSH, NAACP, the Urban League, SCLC, Black United Front, Black Panther Party, and other organizations? I've noticed in running mentoring and rites of passage programs, that in order to keep the men in the program, you have to make them feel important. If a person joins an organization and comes to feel that the program could run without them, there's a very good chance that they will not belong very long.

Another lesson that we need to learn about organizing is that "people join people, not organizations." So said Reverend Herbert Daughtry, the founder of the National Black United Front. Usually people join an organization because a friend recruited them into it. Even in the exceptional case where a person joins an organization for non-personal reasons, their relationship to other members will largely determine whether they stay or leave. Most Black people leave volunteer groups because of personal conflicts, so the relationships among people in any Black organization should be the primary concern of any organizer. That is a sad commentary, but it is true that there's a greater chance that people will leave an organization, not because of ideological differences, but because of personal conflicts.

Unfortunately, this is seen not only in political organizations, but also in the church. Many pastors tell their new members, "If you think now that you've joined the church, you have left all your problems on the outside, you are sadly mistaken." Some even say, "There is no mess like church mess."

I've also seen the same problems in Africentric organizations. The Bible teaches us in Ephesians 6:12, "We struggle not against flesh and blood, but against principalities and rulers in high places." People who are insecure are obsessed with power. They will rationalize that because they are different from you, they are better than you. In some Africentric organizations, they play the game "Who's Blacker Than

Whom?" Who has an African name? How many times have you been to Africa? Who wears African dress? Who is more knowledgeable about African history? I believe my grandmother in Nacogdoches, Texas, in 1960, understood the Nguzo Saba and Ma'at better than most Africentrists have ever understood them.

In many organizations, we do not know how to forgive. People disagree on an issue and wind up not speaking to each other. Several decades ago, Maulana Karenga and Lerone Bennett coined the term "operational unity." This is something every organization needs to master. If we are discussing ten issues and we disagree on nine, in the spirit of operational unity, put aside the nine differences and work on the one you agree upon.

One of the major problems with African Americans (and we'll discuss this in more detail in the next chapter on Africentricity) is that we confuse unity with uniformity. African Americans may not be aware that Whites don't agree on everything. In the 2000 presidential election, if they had agreed, there would have been no need for three candidates—Bush, Gore, and Nader—to have run. Those were three Whites who had disagreements.

There was a meeting that took place among White leaders in a particular city. They discussed numerous issues, and there was disagreement on many of those issues. Upon conclusion, when it was time for the press conference, they presented themselves as a unified front on the issues they agreed upon. African Americans had a similar meeting, and they also had various disagreements. When it was time for their press conference, it was cancelled because the leadership could not agree on how to present themselves.

# Politics and Organizing

Good leadership has three traits; it is:
1. Collective
2. Diversified
3. Invisible

In contrast, Black leadership is:
1. Individualistic
2. Primarily religious
3. Visible

Our leadership is very visible. Many times you'll hear the question, Who's the Black leader of America? The media will often give Black people two leadership camps to choose between: integrationists and nationalists. The following names consistently pop up in this dilemma:

| Integrationists | Nationalists |
|---|---|
| Douglass | Delaney |
| DuBois | Garvey |
| King | Malcolm |
| Jackson | Farrakhan |

Because our leadership is very visible, the assumption is that if you kill the leader, you kill the movement. If you follow one, you can't follow the other. It has been the last duo, Jesse Jackson, Sr., and Louis Farrakhan, who have had the greatest interaction with each other.

Who is the White leader of America? Because good leadership is invisible, if the president died tonight, it would not create a change in foreign policy, the stock market, or the White agenda for this country. In addition, White leadership is diversified. It comes from church, military, political, economic, and technical communities. Black leadership primarily comes from the church.

I just don't believe ministers have all the answers to solve the problems in Black America. I do believe that the combination of Black leaders from the religious, political, economic, military, and technical communities would be much more effective.

Effective organizers study the enemy. A great military strategist, Sun Zi, once observed, "If one knows the enemy, but knows oneself, one may have an equal chance to win or lose. But if one knows neither oneself or the enemy, one will lose every battle."[22]

One of the problems with African Americans is that we treat people as though they were within our value system. Women make that same mistake with men. When Europeans came to Africa, we did not view them as the enemy. We treated them as within our value system. We felt they were there for breakfast, lunch, dinner, or to visit. We had no idea they wanted the land and the people. It makes no sense to be able to build a pyramid 48 stories high, 755 feet wide, with 2,300,000 stones weighing 3 tons each, perfectly balanced, perfectly right-angled, one of the Seven Wonders of the World, and not be able to defend yourself against a minority that comes in with a gun.

If African people had the technology to build a pyramid, they had the technology to defend themselves. J. Edgar Hoover and the FBI's COINTELPRO program got four of our best leaders: Marcus Garvey, Malcolm X, Martin Luther King, and Huey Newton. I encourage you to read books on J. Edgar Hoover and COINTELPRO to understand the full impact that

# Politics and Organizing

this man and program had against Black organizations and leaders.

Since this book is emphasizing solutions, I believe that four of our greatest political movements were the UNIA, headed by Marcus Garvey; the civil rights movement originating in Montgomery; the election of Harold Washington as mayor of Chicago; and the Million Man March in Washington, DC.

How did Marcus Garvey organize one million Black people without television and the Internet and only limited radio? How did he pack Madison Square Garden in 1920 when he unveiled the red, black, and green liberation flag? We need to study his movement.

How did African Americans in Montgomery, Alabama, shut the city down for 381 days and create alternative transportation? How did African Americans with only 40 percent of the vote elect Harold Washington mayor of the most racist city in the country? How did Louis Farrakhan and the Million Man March Committee organize almost two million Black men to come to Washington, DC, to atone for their sins?

Many times we dwell on our losses and don't energize ourselves with our victories. Those were four great movements in Black history. New York, Montgomery, Chicago, and Washington, DC. Whenever we are discouraged, we need to think about those four movements.

Some feel there is a schism between civil rights leaders and the hip hop movement. In Cincinnati 2003, the civil rights community had a rally, 40 years after the March on Washington, but only 500 people attended and 99 percent of the audience were middle age. In contrast, the Hip Hop Summit had a rally in Houston, January 2004 on Superbowl weekend and attracted over 20,000 young adults. They invited hip hop artists to perform, admission was free—it only required that anyone attending—**register to vote**. They did the same in Los Angeles during NBA all-star weekend. Their objective is to register 2,000,000 before the presidential election. Another organization, the National Hip Hop Political Convention plans to continue empowering the hip hop community. We must merge these two movements. This can be done with listening, mutual respect, operational unity, and the willingness of elders to pass the baton.

The Hip Hop generation did not experience Jim Crow. Issues of importance to this generation are different than those of civil rights activists. Marching, boycotting, and voting for the lesser of two evils is not significant to them. When I listen to them, they share their pain and concern about racial profiling, fatherlessness, police brutality, poverty, the judicial unfairness of crack possession, safety, AIDS, STDs, and an irrelevant school curriculum. Much of rap music describes the concentrated poverty they experienced in their childhood and the lack of positive Black middle class role models in their lives. Rap music not only expresses their pain and joy, but has produced more millionaires than DuBois' talented tenth. Author Kevin Powell says, "Tupac Shakur *dead* is more relevant to poor and struggling young Black people in America than any civil rights leader *alive*.

Beyond organizing movements, we must master organizing events. It disappoints me when I speak at a college on Tuesday night and only 50 people are in attendance. Yet I'll speak the following night at another college and there will be close to 1,000. What did the second college do that the first college did not? Our office sends a sheet to college coordinators to assist them in increasing the turnout for the event. The recommended strategies include the following:

# Politics and Organizing

- Let the students determine the topic, not the leader.
- Have professors require attendance at the lecture.
- Advertise the event to the larger community.
- Provide food, not refreshments, after the event.
- Include fraternities and sororities on the program.
- Have the school choir sing an opening and closing song.
- Include a student rapper on the program.
- Have a party after the lecture, with the admission requirement being lecture attendance.

I never will forget author Leroi Jones in the late 1960s and the Congress of African People; they would conduct parties called soul sessions. On the hour, they would turn on the lights and give a one- to five-minute political speech. They understood that African Americans would attend the party, so they used the party as a way of raising consciousness.

In addition to organizing college students, we need to also find ways to organize and educate parents. My experience has taught me that the same scenario applies. I can speak in one school where 10 parents are in attendance and on the following day speak at another school where almost 500 parents are in attendance. What did one school do that the other school did not? Over my career I have studied the question, and my office now provides the following suggestions for principals trying to organize parents:

1. Let the parents choose the topic.
2. Hire a parent coordinator and provide office space.
3. Don't rely exclusively on flyers. Call parents.
4. Consider having the meeting at the local church or community organization.
5. Give a prize to the class that produces the greatest number of parents.

6. Provide door prizes for parents.
7. Provide child care.
8. Provide transportation.
9. Provide security.
10. Provide food, not refreshments, after the program.
11. Have the children perform before and after the speaker.
12. Let the parents choose the day and time of the meeting.

It concerns me when principals and teachers tell me that parents are apathetic, and yet they chose the time of the meeting, which was most compatible with their schedule. Why should parents have to take off work to attend a parent meeting rather than educators spend more time that day to accommodate parents?

We must organize individuals. Everyone should be a member of an organization. Everyone should volunteer a minimum of two hours per week. Everyone should contribute a minimum of $10 per month. All of us need to read the work of Stokely Carmichael (Kwame Toure), in particular *Ready for Revolution*. Stokely's famous challenge was that everyone needs to join an organization, and if you don't like any organization, create a new one.

Stokely says,

"... without organization there is no way to channel all the energies of all the people who want to work for our betterment and improvement.

... organization is necessary because without it we leave ourselves open to the oppressors' tactics of "divide and conquer" or "divide and rule."

... organization is necessary as a tool to make democratic decisions about our future directions.

... organization is necessary because without it we let issues dictate what direction we go in. The enemy (capitalists) constantly creates issues for us to respond to. The end result is that we go in circles and never really get to the root of the problem.

... organization is necessary because oppressed people have never defeated their oppressors without it.

So clearly lack of effective organization is our greater enemy. What is the nature of the organization we need?

... permanent organization because without it there is no guarantee that the

struggle will continue beyond the current phase. We also need to plan for generations ahead because our development spans forever.

... organization allows for us to correctly interpret the true nature of our oppression and how it affects the political, economic, and cultural reality of our lives and to educate the people as to what we are fighting against and what we are fighting for.

... organization that is capable of mass mobilization when necessary to keep the collective energies of the people working for the right objectives.

... revolutionary organization that seeks a total transformation of society from the backward way of having a privileged few who own and control almost everything to a new kind of society where there is no exploitation of the masses of the people."[23]

I challenge everyone to read the Book of Nehemiah and then return home and rebuild some walls. If our best Black minds do not live, work, spend, volunteer, or invest in the Black community, can it be anything else but a ghetto?

In the powerful book *We Have No Leaders,* Harold Cruse makes a major indictment of Black leadership. At a lecture at Prairieview A&M University, Harold Cruse responded to a question asking him to evaluate Black leaders: "What leaders?

We have no leaders." The student questioner responded by listing the familiar names of the heads of the civil rights organizations, members of Congress, and big city mayors. Cruse, responding with evident irritation, said that those persons were not leaders because they had no plan, no program of action, and no organization to mobilize or lead Blacks in a direction that would deal with their communal problems.[24]

That's my challenge to the Black Leadership Roundtable and Forum, the Congressional Black Caucus, and the Congress of National Black Churches. What is your plan? What is the agenda? I've laid out two programs that I want you to consider. The first, how can we save $16 billion to build four regional hotels and acquire corporate jets? The second is to institute an independent Black political party so that we can leverage 24 million votes. The larger White community would then have to respect us. We can no longer vote 92 percent Democratic with no promises for a Black-benefiting agenda. Al Sharpton has given us the challenge. The Democratic Party can no longer treat us like a mistress instead of a spouse. If they do not want to respect us and treat us as equals, then it is time for a divorce. We will no longer allow ourselves to be screwed by the Democrats.

# CHAPTER 8

# POST-TRAUMATIC SLAVERY DISORDER/ AFRICENTRICITY

We use the word trauma in everyday language to mean a highly stressful event. The key to understanding trauma is that it refers to extreme stress that overwhelms a person's ability to cope. The definition of trauma is fairly broad. It includes responses to powerful one-time incidents like accidents, natural disasters, crimes, surgeries, deaths, and other violent events. It also includes responses to chronic or repetitive experiences such as child abuse, neglect, combat, urban violence, concentration camps, battering relationships, and enduring deprivation.

Trauma is defined by the experience of the survivor. Two people could undergo the same noxious event. One person might be traumatized while the other person remains relatively unscathed. It is not possible to make blanket generalizations such as event X is traumatic for all who go through it, or event Y is not traumatic because no one was physically injured.

In addition, the specific aspects of an event that evoke a traumatic reaction will be different from one individual to the next. You cannot assume that the details or meaning of an event, such as a violent assault or rape, that are most distressing for one person will be equally distressing for another.

Many times the media will try to belittle the impact that racism has had on African Americans by illuminating those great people within our race. It reminds me of a track race where the White runner had a fifty-yard head start and the Black runner won. Paul Robeson used his moments of glory to indict the White race rather than boast his greatness. The assumption was that the White race was fair and there was no need for African Americans to complain because the Whites usually won.

In trauma, we must understand that the long stressors deliberately inflicted on people are far harder to bear than accidents or natural disasters. Most people who seek mental health treatment for trauma have been victims of purposely inflicted wounds dealt by another person. If this was done deliberately in the context of an ongoing relationship, the problems are increased. The worst situation is when injury is caused deliberately within a relationship by a person on whom the victim is dependent.

Racism is a prime example of such a relationship. African Americans have been segregated by "for colored only" signs, denied entrance and admission, hosed down by police, spit on, chased by dogs, raped, beaten, castrated, lynched, etc., not to mention having had families split asunder by the slave trade first and later by social inequities.

Trauma might result in the following symptoms:
1.   A state of anxiety, dissatisfaction, or restlessness
2.   Chronic suicidal preoccupation
3.   Self-injury
4.   Explosive or extremely inhibited anger (one of 21 African American males is the victim of homicide)

# Post-Traumatic Slavery Disorder/ Africentricity

5.   Compulsive or extremely inhibited sexuality (68 percent of African American children are born out of wedlock)
6.   Amnesia
7.   Denial (I'm not African, I was born in Mississippi)
8.   Sense of helplessness or paralysis of initiative
9.   Shame, guilt, and self-blame
10.  Sense of defilement or stigma
11.  Substance dependence and abuse (African Americans constitute 12 percent of the U.S. population but consume 38 percent of cigarettes and 39 percent of alcohol)
12.  Preoccupation with relationships with perpetrators (African American males enjoy a three-to-one Black female to male ratio and express their satisfaction with a three to-one-ratio of marrying outside the race)
13.  Revenge
14.  Unrealistic attribution of total power to perpetrator (e.g., spending 96 percent of their money with White businesses)
15.  Isolation and withdrawal
16.  Disruption of intimate relationships (66 percent divorce rate)
17.  Persistent distrust
18.  Loss of sustaining faith
19.  Sense of hopelessness and despair

The long-term after effects of the Jewish Holocaust trauma are far reaching. More than half a century after the war, the Holocaust continues to make its presence felt on survivor families and others in a variety of ways. The National Israeli Center for Psychosocial Support of Survivors of the Holocaust in the Second Generation is a nonprofit organization founded in 1987 and is dedicated to providing such healing. Why did it take more than 40 years after the end of the war to establish such an organization? Many reasons may be suggested. A new social awareness of the Holocaust began to develop in 1960. Having been silent for decades, more survivors than ever were ready to speak out, and they began openly to share their memories and their common mental suffering. While survivors seemed to live a normal life on the outside, their families knew of their private and largely concealed suffering. Ward Connerly and Clarence Thomas are prime African Americans in denial about their trauma. Starting modestly in Jerusalem, the organization today employs about 130 mental health professionals who provide services to thousands of clients.

What about the 36 million African Americans in hundreds of cities across the United States who are presently suffering from post-traumatic slavery disorder? As a consultant to many school districts nationwide, it always amazes me that American educators know that six million Jews died in Europe, but do not know how many Africans died in the United States during slavery.

How is it that we know German history better than we know American history, which relates to African Americans? We need the Association of Black Psychologists to establish offices in every major United States city. They need to be properly funded, either from within the Black community or via reparations. If every African American received thousands of dollars via reparations, but had not been psychologically healed, the money would evaporate in a short period of time. As much as I value economics, the number one problem affecting African Americans is not economics: **it's post-traumatic slavery disorder.**

# Post-Traumatic Slavery Disorder/ Africentricity

Affluent Whites who are valued in America and who have experienced trauma are given treatment immediately. When there have been stressful events—Columbine, Kentucky, Oregon—the government sent counselors immediately to address survivors' needs. The fundamental problem for African Americans is that when slavery ended in 1865, African Americans were not given counseling to address post-traumatic slavery disorder.

Some of the symptoms of this disorder are as follows:
- Associating being smart with acting White
- Believing Blacks are better in sports than science, music than math, rap than reading
- Niggeritis
- Lack of unity
- Crab theory (pulling each other down)
- Defining good hair as long and straight
- Defining pretty eyes as anything but dark brown
- Believing the lighter your hue, the prettier you are
- Believing Jesus Christ looks like Michelangelo's cousin

Na'im Akbar, in the powerful book *Breaking the Psychological Chains of Slavery*, provides additional illustrations of post-traumatic slavery disorder:
- Associating work with slavery
- Devaluing property
- Obsession with materialistic possessions, i.e., cars, clothes, and jewelry
- Not supporting Black leadership
- Stud (males as baby-maker sperm donors)
- Defining Blackness through sports and entertainment

The Swahili word for holocaust is Maafa. I'm suggesting that Black psychologists open Maafa Healing Centers in every major city in America. The fundamental problem is that many

145

African Americans who are suffering from post-traumatic slavery disorder are in denial and do not feel a need to expose themselves to Africentricity, which is needed for their healing.

This chapter could be an entire book, and, indeed, there have been numerous books written on this subject. I recommend the following books for those desirous of healing.

**Adults**

*The Destruction of Black Civilization* by Chancellor Williams

*African Origins of Western Civilization* by Cheikh Anta Diop

*Nile Valley Contributions to Civilization* by Anthony Browder

*Afrocentricity* by Molefi Asante

*Miseducation of the Negro* by Carter G. Woodson

*Breaking the Chains of Psychological Slavery* by Na'im Akbar

*Race Code War* by Khari Enaharo

*Isis Papers* by Frances Welsing

*Slavery: The African American Psychic Trauma* by Sultan and Naimah Latif

*Yurugu* by Marimba Ani

*The Maroon Within Us* by Asa Hilliard

*Peculiar Institution* by Kenneth Stampp

*Shades of Black* by William Cross

*Souls of Black Folks* by W.E.B. DuBois

*United Independent Compensatory Code* by Neely Fuller

**Youth**

*Lessons from History* by Jawanza Kunjufu

*SETCLAE Kindergarten Through Twelfth Grade* by Jawanza Kunjufu and Folami Prescott Adams

*Kids Guide to African American History* by Nancy Sanders

*Holocaust for Beginners* by E. Anderson

# Post-Traumatic Slavery Disorder/ Africentricity

Molefi Asante provides us with a definition of Africentricity. "It is a mode of thought and action in which the centrality of African interests, values, and perspectives predominate. In regards to theory, it is the placing of African people in the center of any analysis of African phenomena."

Listed below are Africentric exercises for Maafa healing: Exercise 1: Every adult should read, meditate, and analyze the Willie Lynch letter. Every parent and teacher should have their child and student do likewise.

> Gentlemen, I greet you here on the banks of the James River in the Year of Our Lord 1712. First, I shall thank you, the gentlemen of the colony of Virginia, for bringing me here. I am here to help you solve some of your problems with slaves.
>
> Your invitation reached me on my modest plantation in the West Indies while experimenting with the newest and still oldest methods for control of slaves. Ancient Rome would envy us if my program is implemented. As our boat sails south on the James River named for the illustrious King James whose Bible we cherish, I find enough to know that your problem is not unique.
>
> While Rome used cords of wood as crosses for standing human bodies along the old highways in great numbers, you are here using the tree and rope on occasion. I caught the whiff of a dead slave hanging from a tree a couple of miles back. You are not only losing valuable stock by hangings, you are having uprisings. Slaves are running away. Your crops are sometimes left in the field too long for maximum profit. You suffer occasional fires. Your animals are killed.
>
> Gentlemen, you know what your problems are. I do not need to elaborate. I am here to provide a method of controlling your black slaves. I guarantee every one of you that installed correctly it will control the slave for at least 300 years. My method is simple. Any member of your family or any overseer can use it.

I have outlined a number of differences among the slaves and I take these differences and make them bigger. I use fear, mistrust, and envy for control purposes. These methods have worked on my modest plantation in the West Indies and they will work throughout the South.

Take this simple little list of differences and think about them. On the top of my list is age, but it is there only because it starts with the letter A. The second is color or shade. There is intelligence, size, sex, size of plantation, attitude of owners, whether the slave lived in the valley, on the hill, east, west, north, south, has fine or coarse hair or is tall or short.

Now that you have a list of differences, I shall give you an outline of action. But before that I shall assure you that distrust is stronger than trust and envy is stronger than adulation, respect, or admiration. The black slave, after receiving this indoctrination, shall carry on and become self-refueling and self-generating for hundreds of years, maybe thousands. Don't forget, you must pitch the old black versus the young black male and the young black male against the old black male. You must use the dark skinned slaves versus the light skinned slaves and the light skinned slaves versus the dark skinned slaves. You must use the female versus the male and the male versus the female. You must also have your servants and overseers distrust all blacks, but it is necessary that your slaves trust and depend on us. They must love, respect, and trust only us.

Gentlemen, these kits are your keys to control. Use them. Have your wives and children use them. Never miss an opportunity. My plan is guaranteed, and the good thing about this plan is that if used intensely for one year, the slaves themselves will remain perpetually distrustful.

In the book *The Peculiar Institution*, author Kenneth Stampp described the four major components that make a slave. They include fear, loyalty, inferiority, and hatred. When you make a slave, the first thing you do is instill fear. Second,

# Post-Traumatic Slavery Disorder/ Africentricity

you teach the slave to only have loyalty toward the master, and you do that by rewarding traitors. Third, you teach them to feel inferior by showing Whites always in authoritative positions. Last, you teach them to hate anything connected to Africa.

Exercise 2: Study the sheep dog. In the powerful book, *The Maroon Within Us*, author Asa Hilliard describes the sheep dog.

> In most places where people raise sheep, a special type of dog with a special type of training is used to watch a flock of sheep. If one of the sheep wanders, the sheep dog will bring him back. This dog will protect the sheep flock from all other animals, including other dogs. When a sheep dog is with its master, it is usually described as loyal, gentle, and intelligent. But the most striking part of the description to me is that the things that are said about the sheep dog's behavior are all from the point of the view of the master and involve the master's needs. The dog's own needs are not really considered other than to determine how these needs may be used by the master to make the dog do what the master wishes. How did this happen? How did a dog come to lose interest in its own independent direction or the direction which as a member of a dog family it is expected to keep? At birth, the puppy is separated almost at once from all the other dogs, brothers and sisters, from its family. It is then placed into a pen where there are nothing but sheep, including the youth lambs who are nursing. In its normal drive to satisfy its hunger, it seeks out an ewe and tries to nurse with her along with other lambs. When it is successful it continues and is then raised with sheep as a lamb until it is sufficiently developed to be trained. Notice here that it continues to look like a dog as well. It will leave the track of a dog and will have the speed and strength of a dog, yet while it has the intelligence of a dog, it will develop the mind of a sheep. Once that happens it no longer acts in the interest of itself as a dog or in the interest of other dogs.[25]

Let us take a moment to review what this story teaches us. For the dog's master to work his will with the dog, he established a training, not an educational process, that had certain key features in it.

- The dog was separated from his family and group at an early age.
- It was continually isolated from them during its learning years.
- It was placed in a sheep's (alien) environment.
- It was fed a sheep's diet.
- It was given a special education.
- It was totally dependent upon the master and never allowed to hunt for itself.
- All the decisions about its training were made outside of its family and without its consultation.

Exercise 3: Watch the *Sankofa* video, and, if possible, visit Ghana and go through the Door of No Return (this door led from the dungeons to the ships). Many psychologists believe that one of the most effective ways to remove the effects of trauma is to take the victim back to where the trauma began. Many of us lost our Africentricity and self-esteem when we went through the Door of No Return. Many of us are now in denial and will make such statements as "I am not African. I was born in Mississippi."

In the excellent book *Shades of Black*, author William Cross describes the Nigrescence model. There are five stages in the model: pre-encounter, encounter, emerging, internalization, and commitment.

# Post-Traumatic Slavery Disorder/ Africentricity

Pre-encounter/Encounter Statements

1. I often say, "Why should I be judged by my race?"
2. I believe that kinky hair doesn't look as nice as straight hair.
3. Knows very little about Black history.
4. A White organization is better than a Black one.
5. I believe straight hair is good hair.
6. Please don't call me African or Black.
7. I hold back my feelings about race.
8. The way some of our people are behaving, we will not be accepted.
9. I think being light or brown is better than being a dark-skinned person.
10. I sometimes feel that Black people are inferior to White people.
11. My goal in life is to make it for myself.
12. I feel it is important to speak good English.
13. I just want to be seen as an individual and a human being.
14. If you are going to make it, you have to learn how to take the Man's insults and keep trying.
15. I get disgusted by the loudness of some of our people.

Emerging Statements

1. I'm feeling and acting as though I have blind faith in Blackness.
2. My anger runs deep, and I have been having daydreams in which I see myself killing White people.
3. I seem to be placing labels on everybody, such as "He's an Uncle Tom," "She's middle class," "He's counterrevolutionary," or "She's bourgeois."
4. The way I dress, my hairstyle, and other symbols of Black militancy are extremely important to me.

5. I feel very defensive about my level of Blackness.

6. I tend to be rather critical and short-tempered with practically all White people as well as with Black people who are not together.

7. Confrontation, bluntness, and an either-or approach describe the way I talk to people about racial issues.

8. I feel social pressure to be Blacker than I am. I act in a rather Blacker-than-thou manner.

9. To me, nothing that is White is good, and everything of value must be Black.

10. I am so angry you could probably measure my Blackness by the level of hatred I feel toward White people.

11. My thoughts are rather rigid. I tend to think in absolute terms, and my ideology has an either-or quality.

12. My emotions are like an exciting sea of Blackness. It is such a wonderful feeling it makes me want to shout to the world, "I'm Black and I'm proud."

13. My body is full with anger, pride, and energy. I feel ready to do whatever is necessary for liberation.

14. I'm thinking about Black liberation almost all the time, and it's difficult for me to concentrate on anything else.

15. I feel as though I'm being covered all over with Blackness, and at the same time my mind and body are being washed of all Whiteness.

16. I act and feel as if I've lost all fear and would do anything for Black liberation.

Internalization and Commitment Statements

1. It is easy for me to criticize Blackness without feeling like a traitor to the cause.

2. I take criticism of the Black movement without getting angry or defensive.

# Post–Traumatic Slavery Disorder/ Africentricity

3.   I can deal with persons on a Blacker-than-thou ego trip without feeling defensive or shaky myself.
4.   I feel like I'm living my Blackness rather than trying to prove it to someone.
5.   My ideology is flexible.
6.   According to the way I act and feel, it would be easy for someone to conclude that my Blackness is based on pro-Black ideas rather than anti-White concepts.
7.   My anger and rage is moderate to low, while my level of Blackness is high.
8.   I am patient and understanding toward people who do not have my level of awareness.
9.   Certainly I wish the revolution was possible, but I feel the struggle for Black liberation will take years of dedicated work.
10.  I am confident, nondefensive, and at ease with my own personal sense of Blackness.
11.  It is very clear to me that some ideas of Blackness are good while others need to be rejected.
12.  I feel at ease and comfortable with my level of Black awareness.[26]

Exercise 4: Compare a picture of Halle Berry and Whoopi Goldberg, and look at them until you believe that Whoopi looks as good as Halle. What are the benefits of dark skin? What are the benefits of a broad nose and thick lips? What are the benefits of short curly hair? Watch the videos from BET, VH-1, and MTV and count the number of African American females that are darker than African American males.

View a portrait of a White image of Jesus and a Black image of Jesus and a poster that says "we worship Him in spirit and in truth." Look at the three posters until you have moved from a White image to a Black image to no image at all.

Exercise 5: Do you know more African history before or after 1619? Write the historical African event next to each year.

3100 BC
2780 BC
2000 BC
1232 BC
800 BC
1619
1865
1920
1954
1968

There's an historical law that says, "When you start will determine where you end." If you start in 1619, you start on a plantation. If you start five thousand years ago, you start on a pyramid. Internalize the ideas that Egypt is in Africa, Africans built the pyramids, and Imhotep is the father of medicine.

Exercise 5: Operational Unity. In the previous chapter we discussed this principle. In the spirit of operational unity, we must put aside our differences and work on similarities. In addition, we must practice the principle of forgiveness. Take a moment and write down all the people that you have a grievance with and have not spoken to or hold some level of resentment and hostility toward. I want you to call, apologize, and forgive them.

# Post-Traumatic Slavery Disorder/ Africentricity

Exercise 6: Can you answer these questions from our SETCLAE curriculum?

1. Who am I?
2. Where did my people originate?
3. When did the history of my people begin?
4. What have my people contributed?
5. What is the culture of my people?
6. Who oppressed my people?
7. How are my people oppressed?
8. How did my people respond?
9. What is the present condition of my people?
10. What can I do to enhance the condition of my people?

Exercise 7: Study and internalize the following statements:

1. Power concedes nothing without a struggle.
2. Until you understand White supremacy, everything else will confuse you.
3. Think Black first.
4. Is it in the best interest of Black people?
5. The greatest good for the greatest number.

Exercise 8: Look at your checkbook and put an A next to the African American businesses that you paid money to and put an F next to the non-African American businesses. What percent of your monthly budget is spent with African American businesses? Set a goal to spend at least 20 percent of your income with African American businesses.

During the O.J. Simpson trial, Johnnie Cochran was accused of using the "race card." I have seen numerous African

American customers play the same card with African American businesses. If the business makes one mistake, they play the card. They are quick to tell the owner they want to support them but …. They also say they would support the brother if his prices were cheaper. Where is the support? If you need their prices to be cheaper, that is not support, that is a benefit to you. Black businesses need your support until their volume equals that of larger businesses. They also use the race card to negotiate for lower prices. I have never seen them play the race card with a White business. People who hate themselves only allow Black businesses to make one mistake before they are scandalized in the larger Black community. These same people are oblivious to White businesses' mistakes and do not generalize if one makes a mistake. Are you guilty of the above? In order to heal, stop playing the race card. If you see a Black business doing wrong, don't slander them and write them off; give them constructive criticism, and continue your support.

Exercise 9: Study Karenga's Kawaida and internalize the principles of the Nguzo Saba and Ma'at. Review the following principles and determine what you can do in a tangible way to illustrate your understanding:

Nguzo Saba
1. Unity
2. Self-determination
3. Collective work and responsibility
4. Cooperative economics
5. Purpose
6. Creativity
7. Faith

# Post-Traumatic Slavery Disorder/ Africentricity

Ma'at
1. Truth
2. Justice
3. Order
4. Harmony
5. Balance
6. Reciprocity
7. Righteousness

Exercise 10: Answer the following questions.

- Do you like the texture of your hair?

- Would you like to be a lighter hue?

- How do you feel about Africa?

- Would you like to visit?

- Would you like to relocate?

- Do you know more Black history before or after 1619?

- How do you feel watching documentaries about slavery and Jim Crow?

- What percentage of your income goes to African American businesses?

- How do you feel about Black men dating White women?

- How do you feel about Black women dating White men?

- Do you associate being smart with acting White?

- Would you send your son to Morehouse or Harvard?

# Post-Traumatic Slavery Disorder/ Africentricity

- Would you send your daughter to Spelman or Yale?

- How do you feel about Ebonics?

- Could you work for a Black supervisor?

- What is your image of God?

- Describe your ideal residential neighborhood?

- How do you feel about most rap videos?

- What is Black culture?

- How do you feel when you are the only African American in the group?

- Would you like to be White?

- Why do Whites control most of the world?

- What is your definition of freedom?

- What is the number one problem facing Black America?

In order for us to effectively implement the solutions that have been provided for Black America, we need to recover from post-traumatic slavery disorder. It is my desire that all of us read the books that have been mentioned and immerse ourselves in Maafa Healing exercises.

I believe that we can create a strong Black economy, be respected as a political bloc, and produce strong academically gifted children and families if we take this chapter seriously. I encourage all readers to use these ideas to create Maafa Healing Centers.

# Post-Traumatic Slavery Disorder/ Africentricity

In the next chapter we will look at the Black church. It is such a major institution in the Black community, that it needs its own chapter.

# CHAPTER 9

# THE BLACK CHURCH

As a born again Christian, who's been washed by the Blood and filled with the Holy Spirit, who loves Jesus more than anyone else, I would be remiss in a book of solutions for Black America, if I did not look at the largest and most significant institution within the Black community.

From an historical perspective, the first Christian church in the world was the Ethiopian Coptic Church. If we look at the African experience during slavery, it was a personal relationship with Jesus Christ that inspired the Nat Turner, Denmark Vessy, and 244 other slave revolts. Racism inspired Richard Allen in 1787 to start the first A.M.E. (African Methodist Episcopal) church.

In the early 1900s, it was Marcus Garvey and the African Orthodox Church that spearheaded the freedom movement. During the 1950s and 1960s, it was the Black church that was the focal point and launch pad for the civil rights era. This is why many non-Christian activists try to have their meetings in the church: because the church has the people.

There are an estimated 85,000 African American churches in Black America. They have $50 billion in assets. They receive $3 billion annually. The conservative estimate is that 40 percent of African Americans are Christians, or 14.4 million out of our 36 million population. Others project the figure to be 60 to 75 percent. These figures include Christians who only attend church on Easter, Mother's, and Father's Day. There are others who claim Jesus when they are in trouble. Others believe in Jesus, but do not feel the need to attend church.

The Black church is not monolithic. You cannot place 85,000 Black churches into one category. The average Black church has 400 members, consisting of 200 adult women, 80 adult men, 80 girls, and 40 boys. In my book *Adam, Where Are You?: Why Most Black Men Don't Go to Church,* we looked at the reality that most churches are two-thirds female and one-third male. Not only is there disparity between adult women and men, there's also a disparity between girls and boys.

In that book, we provide 21 reasons why Adam, Sr., is not in church, but what explains why Adam, Jr., is not present? In my book *Countering the Conspiracy to Destroy Black Boys,* I raise the questions, Do some mothers raise their daughters and love their sons? Do some mothers make their daughters go to church and not their sons? Later in the chapter, we will look at a particular church that has found ways to increase the percentage of African American men in their congregation.

There are three types of churches in Black America: entertainment, containment, and liberation.

In entertainment churches, the pastor hoops and hollers. The congregation dances and shouts. If you ask the members after service or any time during the week what the sermon was about, they would be hard pressed to remember what was said.

Containment churches are primarily only open on Sunday. They are closed throughout the week. They have little impact on the community. It is a sad commentary when you have several once-a-week storefront churches on the block, and their neighbors are liquor stores and drug dealers.

Liberation churches are open five to seven days a week. They have a greater percentage of young people and men in their church. They realize that churches cannot grow with just elders and women. They combine both a preaching and

# The Black Church

teaching ministry. They are also committed to making a difference in the community.

In Numbers 13, Moses sends 12 spies into the promised land of Canaan to observe the land and its inhabitants. Ten of the spies, or 84 percent (entertainment and containment), come back with a bad report. They say the inhabitants are giants and that it would be impossible for the Jews to take over the land, which is wilderness. Two of the spies, Joshua and Caleb, or 16 percent (liberation), say, "We are well able to overcome them." The Lord has promised them the land. It should have taken them 40 days to travel from Egypt to Canaan, but, unfortunately, it took 40 years.

One of the problems in the church is that 84 percent of the churches are still preaching "wilderness," and only 16 percent are preaching "Promised Land." One of the major reasons why so many churches are in the wilderness is because they are deep in debt. It is very difficult for churches to do ministry when a large portion of their budget goes to their mortgage payments.

One of the reasons why the church is in debt is because its members are in debt. Congregations and churches mirror one another. Unfortunately, only 26 percent of Christians are tithers. Will a man rob God? Oh, yes he will! In tithes and in offerings. In Joshua 7, Joshua and his men have just won a difficult battle at Jericho. The next battle is to be easy, at Ai. Unfortunately, they lose that battle and Joshua is frustrated. He asks the Lord, "Why?" The Lord tells him, "One of your men kept the spoils, which I told you not to do." Joshua found out that it was Aiken who had kept the spoils.

The Bible says that the church should be a place of miracles. Could one of the reasons why the church is not operating at full capacity be that 74 percent of their members are robbing God? I'm sure this is why my pastor, Bill Winston, at Living

Word Christian Center, established the rule that only tithers can be members of the church.

From a carnal perspective, I know you're wondering, how can anyone administer that? It's very easy. If the rules say that only tithers can be members, then Living Word Christian would not be affected by any of its members who are non-tithers, obstructing miracles.

How did Creflo Dollar and World Changers Ministry move into an 8,000-seat sanctuary debt free? I wonder how many chicken dinners were sold, fish fries conducted, raffle tickets peddled, etc? The answer is none. They were able to move into their sanctuary debt free because of the large percentage of their members who are tithers. As a result, World Changers Ministry can now allocate its entire budget to ministry and not to mortgage payments.

In the previous chapter, on post-traumatic slavery disorder, I mentioned the impact a White, blonde, blue-eyed image of Jesus Christ has had on the Black psyche. In many entertainment and containment churches, you see this White image on window panes, church hand fans, Sunday school books, and even the cross. This is one of the major reasons why many men do not attend church. It has been said that Christianity is a White religion, that its origins are in Europe, and that Africans received Christianity in 1619 after being transported to America.

Two of the best churches in Black America, to correct this myth, are Trinity United Church of Christ in Chicago, Illinois, and the Shrine of the Black Madonna, located in Detroit, Atlanta, and Houston. If you visit any of these churches, just looking at their sanctuary and their murals will tell the story and make your heart proud. The model and theme of Trinity is "unashamedly Black and unapologetically

Christian." These churches make it clear that the Garden of Eden story is an African story.

The Pishon River is the White Nile, and the Gihon is the Blue Nile. The Garden of Eden story is an African story. Moses was an African (Exodus 2:19). Paul was an African (Acts 21:38). When Herod was looking for Jesus, Joseph hid his son in Egypt. You could not have hidden a White male in Egypt during that era. If you must portray Jesus, should we believe Michelangelo or read Daniel 7:9 and Revelation 1:14-15. Jesus had hair the texture of wool and feet the color of bronze.

Ideally, we should worship Him in spirit and in truth. One of the challenges in the church is that often the truth is not told. Returning to Numbers 13, God promised the land to the Hebrews, but they allowed themselves to be talked out of their promise by 10 leaders who gave a negative report.

I love talking to God, and I have asked him over the years, "Why did you talk to Adam first when you saw that Eve ate the fruit first." God reminded me in Genesis 2:16-17 that He did not give the instructions to Eve. He gave the instructions to Adam, and He holds men accountable for their families.

The same is true for pastors and leaders. I've also asked God, "Why was Moses not allowed to enter into the Promised Land?" He endured Hebrew foolishness and the people's desire to return to Egypt and slavery. God showed me Numbers 26, where He told Moses to speak to the rock. On this particular occasion, Moses, rather than following the instructions, hit the rock instead of speaking to it. That was enough for God to tell Moses that he would not enter into the Promised Land.

God holds his pastors, leaders, and followers to a higher standard. I am aware that parishioners cannot go any further than their leaders. I never will forget the time I went to a marital retreat and the pastor prayed over me in tongues. I rejected what he did. That was because I had never been taught that speaking in tongues is part of your heavenly language and its power. It was only with new leadership that I was able to appreciate the power of speaking in tongues.

When we talk about worshipping Jesus in spirit and in truth, one of the distinctions that can be made among churches is the difference between preaching churches and teaching churches. Many preaching churches will say that they're a combination of the two. The reality is that in preaching churches, a good percentage of the members do not bring their Bibles. The few scriptures that are offered will be in the bulletin. As I mentioned earlier, members of these churches usually cannot remember what the sermon was about just hours later. They also want their pastors to pray for them because they believe pastors have a better connection, perhaps even God's cell phone number.

I mentioned earlier that only 26 percent of Christians are tithers. Do you believe the other 74 percent needs to hear another sermon to become tithers? In the Black community we have the best preachers in the world. Sermons, preaching, hollering, hooping, and sweating seldom change behavior. Meditating on the Word day and night changes behavior.

I've heard ministers preach Job 1:29-31, where it says the Lord giveth and the Lord taketh away. Job 13:15 says, "Though He slay me, yet will I trust Him." I have heard ministers eulogizing an infant who died in his crib say, "The Lord giveth and the Lord taketh away." A teenager was a victim of a drive-by shooting, and we hear "The Lord giveth and the Lord taketh away." A devout young Christian mother dies of breast cancer and again, "The Lord giveth and the Lord taketh away."

# The Black Church

Why would people listening to that message want to worship a God who acts like that? Why would any child love a parent who, thou he slay me, yet will I trust him? Unfortunately, that is one of the faulty reports that we hear. God didn't say that, Job did. Satan comes to kill, steal, and destroy. God comes to give you life and to give you life more abundantly. We need to learn our Father's voice.

One of the major reasons why there are so many people outside of the church is because they don't see much difference in churchgoers' behavior nor their fruit. The divorce rate is almost the same in or outside of the church. Fornication, adultery, homosexuality, and numerous other sins are rampant in both regions.

In the previous chapter on post-traumatic slavery disorder and Africentricity, I emphasized how important identity is, that if you do not know who you are, you will not know what to do with your life. One of the major reasons our people act Eurocentric is because they have not been taught Africentricity. They do not believe they are an African people.

The same is true in the church. There are many leaders who still teach their members that they are sinners saved by grace. That is an oxymoron. If you're saved by grace, you're no longer a sinner. The Bible says you are a saint. Nowhere in the Bible does it refer to believers as sinners saved by grace. Please do not misquote me. I did not say saints do not sin, but there is a distinction between a noun and a verb. Saint is a noun; sin is a verb. To define yourself as a sinner continues to place you in that behavior. Saints understand that they are the righteousness of God, and their righteousness is not based on something they earn. It is based on their relationship to Him. The Bible reminds us in Romans 8:1, "There is no condemnation for those who are in Christ Jesus."

There is also too much death and sickness in the church. I've preached and taught in hundreds of churches in America, and it concerns me when the sick and shut-in list is almost as long as the church roll. What puzzles me is that right after they review the names on the sick and shut-in list, they mention ham and chitterlings will be served right after service. Is there any connection between their menu and their sick-shut-in list?

Some leaders then use I Timothy 4:4-5 to rationalize their diet: "Every creature is good to eat if it is prayed over and sanctified by the Word of God." Good pastors teach their congregations that you do not take scripture out of context, the matter be established out of the mouths of three witnesses (Deuteronomy 19:15).

Slave owners found one bit of scripture in Ephesians 6 to rationalize slavery. Chauvinistic men found one bit of scripture in Ephesians 5 to rationalize the notion that women must submit and obey. Now we have found one bit of scripture that allows us to eat whatever we want. If we read Genesis 1:29, Leviticus 11, and Daniel 1, we will receive a more comprehensive view of God's dietary wishes for us.

This book is solutions oriented, and I'm trying to identify and lift up those people and institutions that have made a positive contribution to the Black community. Look at the Seventh Day Adventists. Is it an accident that they have the least incidence of heart disease, cancer, diabetes, and fibroid tumors of any denomination? Could their vegetarian diet have any impact on this result?

As we examine some outstanding ministries, let's look at what liberation churches offer.

# The Black Church

1. Sunday worship services
2. Saturday and Sunday evening worship services (not everyone can attend Sunday morning worship)
3. Mid-week worship services
4. Daily Bible study
5. Choir rehearsals
6. Usher, deacon, trustee meetings
7. Women's fellowship
8. Men's fellowship
9. Counseling
10. Singles ministry
11. Couples ministry
12. Scouts
13. Tutoring
14. Rites of passage
15. Employment services
16. Literacy classes
17. Day care
18. Elementary school, high school tutoring
19. Evangelism classes
20. Security
21. New member classes
22. Seniors fellowship
23. Book store
24. Prison ministry
25. Transportation
26. Dance and drama
27. Athletics
28. Local support to businesses
29. Scholarships
30. Bereavement counseling
31. Health counseling

32. Church in society seminars
33. Media relations
34. Substance abuse programs
35. World missions

Entertainment and containment churches offer very little of the above. Many liberation churches offer all of these ministries and more. It disappoints me when so many people outside the church, who do not volunteer or contribute, criticize the church in light of all of the above ministries and their impact on the Black community.

In addition to the fine ministries listed above, there are some ministries that have gone well beyond the call of duty. The Lord is doing miraculous things in their church. Listed below are some of the fine men, women, congregations, denominations, and ministries.

In 1980, Father George Clements founded the One Church One Child Program. There are more than a half-million African American children who are in need of adoption. Many agencies took the position that the Black community was not interested in the adoption of these children. As a result of this excellent ministry, more than 200,000 African American children have been adopted, and the program is now operating in 30 cities nationwide.

In 1994, Father Clements founded the One Church One Addict Program. The impact of drugs on the Black community has been devastating. As a result of the leadership of Father Clements, more than 600 churches have created One Church One Addict programs. There are almost 5,000 addicts who have moved from crack to Christ, liquor to the Lord, and heroin to the Holy Spirit.

# The Black Church

In 1999, Father Clements founded One Church One Inmate. Throughout this book, we have mentioned the 1.5 million African American males and almost 300,000 African American females incarcerated. The recidivism rate is 85 percent. Under the leadership of Father Clements and those progressive churches that have adopted One Church One Inmate, these inmates are not returning to jail, but are living constructive lives.

In 1993, Bishop Henry Williamson founded the One Church One School Program. He was aware that the Black community should be a village and that the education of our children should not be solely borne by educators. He was also aware that a large percentage of teachers are non-African Americans, and many schools are without a male presence. Under Bishop Williamson's leadership, more than 200 churches have adopted schools. Many more churches have done so without formally being members of this great organization.

## Balm In Gilead

This program was founded in 1989. There are now 10,000 churches that have become a part of this organization that is concerned about the devastating impact that AIDS has had on the Black community. As mentioned earlier, 43 percent of male AIDS victims in America are African American, and 64 percent of female AIDS victims in America are African American. The Balm In Gilead ministry is designed to equip churches to become more aware of AIDS and to provide HIV testing and counseling to their members. Unfortunately, there were many churches that initially took the position that AIDS was God's response to a sinful lifestyle and that the victims needed to die.

The first objective of the Balm In Gilead ministry is to have pastors become more sensitive and to make their congregations aware of this epidemic. Because AIDS has had an even more detrimental effect in Africa than in America, with many African children and teens becoming orphans, Balm In Gilead has become a worldwide ministry. While I agree with this ministry in the short-term (education and compassion), condom distribution and condoning homosexuality does not address the long-term root issues of AIDS.

### Youth Ministries

Allen A.M.E. Church in Jamaica, pastored by Floyd and Elaine Flake, have a youth church called Shekinah. I have had the privilege of preaching at Shekinah Church numerous times. I have never seen a youth church quite like Shekinah. Many churches say that their children are their future, but my way of evaluating a church's commitment to children is by looking at what percentage of the budget is allocated to youth? What percentage of the ministries and space is allocated to youth? Unfortunately, in many entertainment and containment churches, children sit in a corner with graham crackers and apple juice during the worship hour. At Allen A.M.E. Church, the youth have their own sanctuary. Have you ever seen 1,000 young people worship Jesus Christ for more than three hours in prayer, scripture, sermon, dance, drama, rap, drill team, poetry, etc.? It is a fantastic experience. Allen A.M.E. also operates one of the best Christian elementary schools in the country.

I also want to acknowledge Greater Christ Baptist Church under the leadership of Pastor James Perkins in Detroit, Michigan, and the creation of the Benjamin E. Mayes Academy. This Academy only teaches male students. While the rest of the country continues to debate single-gender classrooms and single-gender schools and whether or not they violate Title 9 legislation, the Benjamin E. Mayes Academy continues to produce excellent male graduates.

The last church that I want to highlight in the youth category is New Birth, pastored by Bishop Eddie Long. Often you will hear adults express their dissatisfaction with young people hanging on the corners and seemingly having nothing to do and nowhere to go. If adults are serious about their disapproval of young people hanging on corners, then they should provide them with places for recreational activities. New Birth has a Friday Night Explosion. Young people are welcomed at the church from 8:00 p.m. to midnight to play basketball, listen to gospel music, hear clean rap, see Christian and cultural videos, play games, dance, and just enjoy themselves.

Trinity United Church of Christ, pastored by Jeremiah Wright, Jr., and others, also provides similar experiences and youth revivals.

### Economics

Earlier we mentioned that there are 85,000 churches in Black America with $50 billion in assets that receive $3 billion annually. If you divide three billion by 52 weeks, every Monday morning Black churches deposit $57 million in primarily White banks.

In 1993, under the leadership of Pastor Jonathan Weaver at Mount Nebo A.M.E. Church in Maryland, several pastors came together to create the Collective Banking Group. This group now represents 150 churches. They have been able to assemble $100 million in deposits and have leveraged this with banks to create $250 million in loans. The Collective Banking

SOLUTIONS FOR BLACK AMERICA

Group was concerned about the ridiculous reality that Black churches were depositing money into White banks from which their members were not able to secure loans.

My church, Living Word Christian Center, pastored by Bill Winston, has gone a step further with the creation of the New Covenant Bank. If a church has that kind of assets, then why shouldn't the church create its own bank? Smaller churches could combine their resources with other churches to create a bank. Depending upon the state, the financial requirements will range from $2 to $10 million. If you have churches with combined memberships of 20,000 or more members, who by investing in the bank will become its owners, then this becomes a very realizable possibility.

Besides creating the New Covenant Bank, the Living Word Christian Center also created the Joseph School of Business and Entrepreneurship. This school offers a nine-month training program in Christian entrepreneurship. One of the major reasons for the 85 percent Black business failure rate is lack of knowledge in business and Christian principles.

In New York City, the Abyssinia Development Corporation, a project of Abyssinia Baptist Church, spearheaded the creation of the Harlem Center, a $60-million retail and office building. The corporation also brought to the neighborhood various businesses and the construction of a new high school.

In 1986, about 90 religious leaders in Harlem came together to form the Community Improvement Project. The Reverend Johnny Youngblood of St. Paul is one of the organizers of the East Brooklyn Congregations, a collection of churches that have organized and developed initiatives in Brooklyn. He is credited with spearheading the Nehemiah Housing Project, which to date has constructed about 2,500 owner-occupied single-family homes. Windsor Village in Houston, Texas, pastored by Kirbyjon Caldwell, has created the Power Center. They have acquired business office space and have also done housing development.

There are numerous churches that have done similar work. The list is long, but there are three churches in particular that I want to acknowledge. They all are in southern California. One is the Crenshaw Christian Center, pastored by Dr. Fred Price. They employ 350 people and have literally created a city of housing and business developments near their church. Similar activities are conducted by Bishop Kenneth Ulmer and the Faithful Central Bible Church. They not only are involved in numerous business and housing development projects, but they have also acquired the former home of the Los Angeles Lakers. Bishop Ulmer has shown his astuteness and business acumen in that the Forum throughout the week is used for commercial enterprises and on Sunday is reserved for their worship services.

The other outstanding church in the Los Angeles area that I want to acknowledge is First A.M.E. Church, pastored by Chip Murray. Similarly to Pastor Bill Winston's Joseph School of Business, First A.M.E. Church has created a venture capital fund. For many African American business owners, the problem has not been lack of a business plan, but lack of capital. Under the leadership of First A.M.E. Church, the venture capital fund has been able to loan hundreds of African Americans money to start their own businesses.

### Community Involvement

In Chicago, under the leadership of Pastor James Meeks, Salem Baptist Church has done a tremendous job of making an impact in their community. In the Roseland area, within an approximate 100-block radius, there were 34 liquor stores. Under the leadership of Rev. Meeks, Salem was able to have the city of Chicago declare Roseland dry. Do you know how hard it is to declare a Black community dry and exempt from liquor stores? The Bible reminds us that things get done not by might, not by power, but by His Holy Spirit. It takes almost an act of the Holy Spirit to declare a Black community dry.

In the earlier "Family and Health" chapter, I mentioned that African Americans, who comprise only 12 percent of the population, earn only 3 percent of the income, but buy 39 percent of the alcohol. In addition to that feat, Salem determined that there were 46,000 inmates in Illinois prisons. They felt the best form of rehabilitation is to understand God's Word. Every Illinois inmate received a Bible. Also, every Thursday evening, Salem's prayer teams hold prayer parties on every block in Roseland. Lastly, they not only have adopted schools within their zip code, but every child in their zip code is eligible to receive tutoring from Salem. There has been a major improvement in test scores.

Azusa in Boston, Massachusetts, pastored by Reverend Eugene Rivers, has created the 10 Point Boston Miracle. More than a decade ago, Reverend Rivers was concerned about the large number of homicides in Boston. In the Black community alone, there were 62 youth homicides. As a result of Azusa, the Ella Baker House, Reverend Rivers, and others have reduced homicides 200 percent by patrolling the streets, mentoring young people, teaching them the Word of God, providing employment assistance and tutoring, and working in collaboration with the police department. The 10 Points are listed below:

# The Black Church

- Establish four- or five-church cluster collaborations to sponsor "Adopt-A-Gang" programs that organize and evangelize youth gangs. Inner-city churches would serve as drop-in centers and provide sanctuary for troubled youth.

- Commission missionaries to serve as advocates and ombudsmen for Black and Latino juveniles in the courts. Such missionaries would work closely with probation officers, law enforcement officials, and youth street workers to assist at-risk youth and their families. They would also convene summit meetings among school superintendents, principals of public, middle, and high schools, and Black and Latino pastors to develop partnerships that focus on the youth most at-risk. We propose instituting pastoral work with the most violent and troubled young people and their families. In our judgment this is a rational alternative to ill-conceived proposals to substitute incarceration for education.

- Commission youth evangelists to do street-level one-on-one evangelism with youth involved in drug trafficking. Young evangelists would also work to prepare these youth for participation in the economic life of the nation. Such work might include preparation for college, the development of legal revenue-generating enterprises, and acquisition of trade skills and union membership.

179

- Establish accountable, community-based economic development projects that go beyond "market and state" visions of revenue generation. Such an economic development initiative would microenterprise projects, worker cooperatives, and democratically run community development corporations.

- Establish links between suburban and downtown churches and frontline ministries to provide spiritual, human resource, and material support.

- Initiate and support neighborhood crime-watch programs within local church neighborhoods. If, for example, 200 churches each covered the four corners surrounding their sites, 800 blocks would be safer.

- Establish working relationships between local churches and community-based health centers to provide pastoral counseling for families during times of crisis. We also propose the initiation of drug abuse-prevention programs and abstinence-oriented educational programs focusing on the prevention of AIDS and sexually transmitted diseases.

- Convene a working summit meeting for Christian Black and Latino men and women in order to discuss the development of Christian brotherhoods and sisterhoods that would provide rational alternatives to violent gang life. Such groups would also be charged with fostering family responsibility and protecting houses of worship.

# The Black Church

- Establish rape crisis drop-in centers and services for battered women in churches. Counseling programs must be established for abusive men, particularly teenagers and young adults.

- Develop an aggressive Black and Latino curriculum, with an additional focus on the struggles of women and poor people. Such a curriculum could be taught in churches as a means of helping our youth understand that the God of history has been and remains active in the lives of all people.

In Cincinnati, Ohio, New Prospect Baptist Church, pastored by Damien Lynch III, has done similar work as Azusa. They not only patrol the streets, but they bring adults, youth, and the homeless back to the church for evening worship services. Cincinnati has been a hotbed of police brutality. The city literally has sometimes been on lockdown. Under the leadership of Pastor Lynch, they have been able to successfully boycott the city and negotiate their demands.

Father Michael Pfleger, of St. Sabina Catholic Church in Chicago, has historically been concerned about the billboards in the Black community that promote alcohol and cigarettes. Under his leadership, the community has either put pressure on the advertisers to remove those billboards or they have painted them over. In addition, they are concerned about stores selling drug paraphernalia. Father Pfleger and his congregation visit those stores and protest until they remove those items.

The last church in this category is pastored by Deron Cloud. It was founded in 1995, and it goes under several names: Church of the Lord's Disciples, Soul Factory, and the Soldiers

Ministries. This is one of the most dynamic churches I've ever preached in or experienced. The church has three locations in the Washington-Maryland area. Although just seven years old, only time will tell the success of this ministry. In a short period of time, Rev. Cloud has taught his congregation that they are soldiers for Christ. A major focus is reaching out to the least of these, primarily males who have been homeless, incarcerated, and unemployed.

### Personal Development

In Houston, Texas, under the leadership of Pastor I. V. Hilliard, New Light Christian Center created the Life Changes Institute. This is a 90-day residential program for substance abusers. The program receives no government funds. It is solely supported by the church. They are very clear in their belief that the best way to remove someone from drugs is to introduce them to Jesus Christ. To make sure there is no conflict between church and state, the Center itself exclusively finances the program. Their efficacy is 90 percent! This is absolutely fantastic.

Pastor Creflo Dollar in Atlanta, Georgia, and Tony Evans, pastor of Oak Cliff Bible Fellowship in Dallas, Texas, created two excellent programs. Rev. Dollar's program is called Project Joseph. Oak Cliff's program is called Project Turnaround. Both programs have a similar mission. They use comprehensive, church-based, community-impact strategies designed to rebuild lives from the inside out. It is their conviction that true, long-term life transformation must address the moral and spiritual foundations upon which those lives are built, while simultaneously meeting material needs. It is also their conviction that the church, not the government, is the best

# The Black Church

social service delivery system since it is closest to the needs of people, has the largest potential volunteer force, has already existing facilities, and operates on a faith-based, moral frame of reference.

Years ago Oprah Winfrey realized that simply giving people money was not going to significantly turn their lives around. She reached out to the University of Illinois Social Work Department, hoping that they could provide classes for low-income and welfare recipients that would empower them to use her money wisely. If only Oprah Winfrey had reached out to programs like Project Turnaround and Project Joseph.

### Health

Pastor John Cherry, leads the Heart Church Ministries in Maryland, which was founded in 1982. It has grown to more than 26,000 members. They operate many of the ministries mentioned earlier. The ministry I want to highlight here is their Center for Health and Healing that opened in 1999. The purpose of the Center is to improve the health and well-being of their members and the larger community. The Center has grown to include several full-time physicians specializing in pediatrics, obstetrics, gynecology, family practice, and internal medicine. How many churches to do you know that have their own clinics?

Another church I want to identify is pastored by Rev. Wayne Gordon: the Lawndale Community Church in Chicago. It is located in one of the poorest communities in America. Pastor Gordon, like Father Pfleger, is White, pastoring an African American congregation, and doing a mighty work for the Lord. Pastor Gordon lives in Lawndale and realized that one of the major problems in the community was lack of

183

adequate health care. Under his leadership, they have created a clinic of more than 10 physicians and 20 nurses, and they annually provide health care for 80,000 community residents.

Finally, Rev. A. R. Bernard, Sr., pastors the Christian Cultural Center in Brooklyn, New York. Christian Cultural Center is a large liberation church that operates many of the programs previously mentioned. When I released *Adam, Where Are You? Why Most Black Men Don't Go To Church*, I challenged my reading and listening audience to tell me if they knew of one church that had a large percentage of male members. The only church that was offered was Christian Cultural Center. I believe that when you save a man, you save a family. I also believe that men prefer less preaching, hooping, and hollering and more teaching. Pastor Bernard is a teacher. You will often find him using an overhead projector or a flip chart. He wants everyone to fully understand what is being said.

It is now time for the last chapter: "Implementation." At the outset of this book I mentioned that one of my mentors, Dr. Barbara Sizemore, gave me the theoretical paradigm: problem, cause, solution, and implementation. Most of us have a pretty good understanding of the problems. I have tried to point out some of the causes and identify a number of solutions. The challenge in the Black community, however, has been implementation. The church has given us many prime examples of what can be done when good leadership implements programs that are effective. In the last chapter, we will look at other organizations outside of the church and examine what they have done. We will also analyze why implementation has been a difficult challenge.

# CHAPTER 10

# IMPLEMENTATION/ MODELS OF SUCCESS

I am reminded of the Biblical story in Matthew 25, where one steward received five talents, one three, and the other one. Are we in the Black community being good stewards with our talents? Listed below are the assets of Black America.

$688 billion

9,000+ elected officials

900,000+ businesses

85,000 churches with $50 billion in assets, $3 billion annually

4 million college graduates, 2 million college students, 102 + Black colleges

200+ radio stations, 200+ newspapers, 3 television networks

2 million acres of land

84 percent of NBA and 67 percent of NFL athletes

56 percent of musical artists

Have we leveraged these assets properly? Have we been good stewards? Have we gone from theory to practice and implemented solutions?

Robert Woodson, the founder of the National Center for Neighborhood Enterprise organization, in his book The Triumph of Joseph provides the following challenge:

> There are many powerful social, economic, and political institutions that have a proprietary interest in the continued

existence of the problems of the poor, the denial of the existence of solutions, and the portrayal of low-income people as victims in need of defense and rescue. These powerful interest groups include members of the civil rights establishment, a massive poverty industry that owes its existence to the problems of the poor, and politicians who are in line with them. These experts whose careers and celebrity status depend upon the existence of a problem can write about the problem, consult about it, and speak about it on talk shows. They can do everything but solve the problem.[28]

This is a powerful challenge. My question to you is, Is it true? At the outset of the book, I mentioned that my major concern was not the 32 percent of our population that earns more than $50,000 per year, but the 20 percent of our adult population and the 50 percent of our children who live below the poverty line.

One of the organizations that Woodson refers to is the Kennelworth Parkside Housing Organization. In Washington, DC, this public housing organization stands as a dynamic example of what can be accomplished when layers of bureaucracy are removed and real community control is achieved. The community was plagued with violent crime and drug trafficking and was rife with welfare dependency, teen pregnancy, and high school dropouts. The residents of the housing development organized and created their own security patrols to oust drug dealers. They also launched a college preparation program, College Here We Come, through which nearly 600 youth from the development were placed in college within a 12-year period. Within four years of resident management, welfare dependency was reduced by 50 percent, crime fell by 75 percent, and rental receipts increased by 77 percent. A cost/ benefit analysis conducted by an accounting firm

# Implementation/Models
# of Success

projects that cost-efficient management by the residents saved the District government $4.5 million over a 10-year period.[29]

I think MAD DADS is a stellar example of an organization that has moved from theory to practice. MAD DADS started in May 1989 in Omaha, Nebraska. Gang members who wanted to hijack a Jeep Suzuki because it had blue and red colors on it viciously beat John Foster's son, who was home on spring break from college. When Sean finally made it home, beaten and bloody, and told his father what happened, John Foster went to the streets with loaded guns to seek revenge. After looking for hours in vain for his son's attackers, he returned home, reigned in his rage, and turned it into something positive, MAD DADS.

MAD DADS (Men Against Destruction Defending Against Drugs and Social Disorder) is a national nonprofit, nontraditional program designed to mobilize men in the struggle to save youth from guns, drugs, violence, and social disorder. With a genesis of only 18 men in Omaha, MAD DADS has grown to more than 45,000 men nationally, with 52 chapters in 14 states. They perform weekend street patrols within troubled areas. They report crime, drug sales, and other destructive activities to the proper authorities. They paint over gang graffiti and challenge the behavior of drug dealers and gang members. They also provide positive community activities for youth, such as block parties, rallies, night parades, and car shows. They provide chaperones for community events and act as surrogate fathers to youth in nontraditional times and locations. They visit local jails and prisons to counsel and encourage. They also are involved in rites of passage programs. Their program is called Sankofa.

Another organization I want to highlight was founded by Hall of Fame football player Jim Brown. In 1988 he founded the Amer-I-Can Program. A powerful life-management-skills and human-development program, the Amer-I-Can Program emphasizes elevating self-esteem, achieving success through self-determination, and creating an attitude change from "I can't" to "I can." The program consists of a 60- to 90-hour, 15-chapter, life-management-skills curriculum that is designed to empower individuals to take charge of their lives and achieve their full potential. The objective of the program is to cause enrollees to examine their past conditioned behavior patterns and systemically apply proven methods to change behavior that negatively influences their lives.

Under the leadership of Jim Brown, in many cities across America gang violence has been reduced because gang members trust Jim Brown and they respect his program.

I mentioned earlier in the book the great work of Joseph Marshall and the Omega Boys Club. They also patrol the streets and minister to youth. Marshall understands and appreciates youth and hip hop culture, and Omega has earned nationwide accolades.

One of our best organizations is SHAPE (Self-Help for African People Through Education). It was founded in 1969 in Houston, Texas. They offer numerous programs that include tutoring, counseling, food coop, legal assistance, drug treatment, fine arts, rites of passage, and voter registration. They have also been very active fighting police brutality. Another successful organization is Universal founded by record producer Kenny Gamble. In Philadelphia, Universal has begun building 2000 affordable houses, a shopping mall, and a K-12 charter school. Universal's theme is "let's rebuild the ghetto."

What is the plan of Black America? What is our offensive strategy? Throughout this book, reflecting its title, the emphasis has been on solutions. Listed below are most of the solutions, as well as the successful organizations and programs that we have presented throughout this book.

# Implementation/Models
# of Success

Home-schooling
Single-gender classrooms and schools
Ron Edmonds' Effective School model
Teach for Black America
Heritage Foundation No Excuse Schools
KIPP Academy
From Cradle to Classroom
Council of Independent Black Institutions
Financial Support of HCBUs & UNCF
Rule 110
Increase study time, decrease television
Tesa-Education Trust
Saturday academies
Efficacy Committee and the psychology of performance
Comer School Development Program
SETCLAE
NABSE's Pre-referral Intervention Process
MAC Scholars
Minority Student Achievement Network
NAACP's ACT-SO
Welsing's theory 28, 30, 2, and 4
Village Fathers
Institute for Responsible Fathers
Project Alpha
Urban League's Male Responsibility Project
A.C. Green's It Ain't Worth It abstinence program
Mandatory premarital counseling
Clean needle exchange
Tithing
Wealth empowerment seminars
Development School for Youth
Operation Hope
National Foundation for Teaching Entrepreneurship

Matah
Ujamaa
One dollar campaign
$16 billion national conference program
Support Royal Palm Crowne Plaza
Kazi
Blue-collar trade schools
Reparations
Vertical powernomics
National Black Independent Political Party
Hip Hop summit
National Hip Hop political convention
Term limits
Voter registration
Bloc voting
Operational unity
Join and support an organization
Maafa Healing School
Nguzo Saba
Ma'at
Wall Street Project
Collective Banking Group
Creflo Dollar's Joseph Project / Tony Evans' Project
Turnaround
Life Changes Institute
Shekinah
Friday Night Explosion
Rev. Eugene Rivers' Boston 10-Point Miracle
New Covenant Bank
Joseph School of Business
Muhammad Farms, Beulah Land, Republic of New Africa
MAD DADS

# Implementation/Models
# of Success

Amer-I-Can
Nation of Islam
BOND
SHAPE
Omega Boys Club
Kennelworth Parkside Organization
One Church One Child
One Church One School
One Church One Addict
One Church One Inmate
Church clinics
Salem's Outreach Ministries
Balm in Gilead

If we're serious about moving from theory to practice, we need to implement these solutions and emulate these organizations and programs in four target cities—Camden, New Jersey; Compton, California; Benton Harbor, Michigan; and Tunica, Mississippi. Each city represents a region of the United States. They are predominantly African American communities, and they all possess less than 100,000 people. Before we try to make over New York, Chicago, Los Angeles, and Houston, we should attempt to turnaround Camden, Compton, Benton Harbor, and Tunica.

These cities all have next door neighbors that are predominantly White, so the contrast reflects the best and worst of America. In neighboring White cities, the median income is more than $50,000, while in the African American cities, the majority of the people live below the poverty line.

Why is the Black community in its present state? What prevents us from implementing these solutions? Does the White man prevent us from asking each of us to give $1 in order to ultimately raise $36 million to address our problems?

One of the reasons why we have not been effective with implementation and why Cruse may be correct, is that most Black leaders do not have a plan. They have been on the defense. From an athletic and sports perspective, it is difficult to win a game when you are always playing defense and reacting to the opponent. Most Black leaders and organizations have been playing defense and have been reacting to crises.

It reminds me of school principals whose day seldom reflects their objectives. They simply respond to parents, students, and teachers who interrupt them throughout the day. Listed below are some of the crises that have evoked response from Black leadership.

The 2000 presidential election and debacle in Florida
Elections every two years
Justices appointments
Police brutality
State budget deficits
Ward Connerly's Proposition 54
High-stakes testing
Vouchers
Confederate flag
Haiti

Another factor that has kept Black organizations from becoming offensive-minded is their lack of funding and their inferior funding sources. It is difficult for Black organizations to solve the problems of the world without adequate funding. As mentioned in the "Economics" chapter, one of the major reasons why it has been difficult to convince organizations not to meet for one year in order to accumulate investment

# Implementation/Models
# of Success

funds is that organizations are dependent upon their annual national conferences for their financial support.

One of the major reasons why most HCBUs are having financial challenges is because only 16 percent of their alumni contribute. The fiscal solvency of Black colleges should not be solely the burden of Tom Joyner, Bill and Camille Cosby, and John Johnson. Our challenge to every graduate of a Black college is to make an annual contribution to their school.

As I mentioned in the "Black Church" chapter, only 26 percent of Christians are tithers. That explains why the Black Church is in debt and is unable to do more in the area of ministry, as they pay excessive mortgage payments.

Every Saturday morning since 1972, Jesse Jackson, Sr., and Operation PUSH have conducted Saturday rallies. Every Saturday, Jackson tries to put a new twist on the struggle to appeal to the audience to support Operation PUSH and the Rainbow Coalition. Do you know how challenging it is for Jackson every week to come up with another powerful speech that will encourage people to contribute? Operation PUSH experienced tremendous financial challenges when Jackson moved to Washington, DC, to become a shadow senator. For that reason, Jackson tries his best to be in Chicago once a week, regardless of what challenges occur around the world. On those rare occasions when he is outside of Chicago, he attempts to call in and share his telephone conversation with the larger audience.

This reminds me of many pastors who do not let it be known on what Sunday they will be absent because they know their members would turn out in smaller numbers, thus reducing that week's tithes and offerings. This illustrates how many organizations are dependent upon charismatic leadership. As a member and supporter of Operation PUSH, my concern is about the future of the organization when Jesse Jackson, Sr., is no longer available.

As I said in a previous chapter, good leadership is invisible, collective, and diversified. Many organizations, like the National Urban League, that have not had the charismatic leadership of a Jesse Jackson, Sr., are dependent upon grants from the government and the private sector. I encourage all of you to review your support of Black organizations, and then you'll have a better understanding of why we have not implemented known solutions.

It is difficult to implement solutions when you are funded by the Fortune 500 and the government. How can you defeat Pharaoh with Pharaoh's money? I would also like you to review the Jewish Federation to get a better understanding of how only six million Jews in America are able to dominate the banking, media, and legal industries. The Jewish community supports Jewish organizations.

How much money did you contribute to Black organizations last year?

Another reason why we have not been effective in implementing solutions is because many organizations are dependent upon a volunteer base. It is difficult to run an organization when almost all your staff are volunteers. It is even more challenging when most African Americans do not volunteer. We must remember Stokely Carmichael's challenge: All of us need to join an organization.

My challenge in all my speeches has always been, How can you work 40 hours for someone else and not find two hours to volunteer in your community? One of my organizations is Community of Men, which is similar to MAD DADS. Our objective is to stand on drug-infested corners and pass out literature, educating our people on the original sources

# Implementation/Models
## of Success

of guns and drugs. We secured a building where we tutor and mentor boys and teach them rites of passage and entrepreneurship. Often, our men are no shows. As a Christian organization, we pray and hope they return.

I asked members of the National of Islam how they handle members who are no shows. They smiled at me and said, "We prey, not p-r-a-y, but p-r-e-y on the brother." We need to be able to hold each other accountable. We need to take volunteerism seriously. If you promised the organization you're going to volunteer for two hours on a given day at a given time, you need to treat that promise the way you treat your work schedule.

One of the reasons why we have not been effective at implementation is that most of our organizations generalize and do not specialize in a particular area. Many of our organizations, including Operation PUSH, NAACP, Urban League, SCLC, the Political Action Network, and others attempt to solve all the problems in politics, economics, education, etc. Many of our organizations have become Jacks of all trades and specialists at nothing.

I recommend that racism and crises be handled by Operation PUSH, the Nation of Islam, NAACP, and the Political Action Network. Politics should be coordinated by the Congressional Black Caucus and the National Conference of Black Mayors. Economics should be handled by the Urban League, Matah, and the Collective Banking Group. Education should be coordinated by the National Association of Black School Educators, the Council of Independent Black Institutions, Black Child Development Institute, the United Negro College Fund, and the State of Black Education.

Another reason why we've been ineffective at implementation is that we are not clear on the definition of freedom. In the 1960s popular phrases were "the struggle" and "we are involved in the movement." We haven't achieved freedom because many of us define freedom as "the struggle." The struggle cannot be the end goal.

What is your definition of freedom? For some of us, freedom is based on financial security. Thirty-two percent of our race earns in excess of $50,000. Some find less time to volunteer two hours a week and financially support organizations because freedom has now been defined as how many times a week they can play golf, tennis, and bowl. It has been said that you can buy Negroes very cheap. Many can be bought with a good job, house, money, car, or sex.

What is your price? I often think of Harriet Tubman when for the first time in her life she was free to run, play, dance, laugh, study, and pursue a career and family. Why did she return to the South 19 times with a bounty on her head? I have read her works. She said, "How can I be free if my brothers and sisters are not free?" To her, freedom was collective, not individualistic. She also said, "I would have freed more than 300, but the others did not know they were slaves." They thought that living in the master's house was freedom. My definition of freedom is:

- People who love God by obeying His commandments,
- Collective non individualistic,
- We provide our definition of beauty. We determine our images and develop our curriculum. We do not allow other people's perceptions to determine our destiny. Our future is in our hands,
- African Americans who know and appreciate their history, values, and culture; and it is expressed with no to minimal crime,

# Implementation/Models
# of Success

- Thriving Black communities that possess African American businesses that employ millions of African Americans,
- A tremendous reduction in our divorce and fatherless rate,
- No racial profiling, redlining, job glass ceilings, or any other form of racial discrimination,
- All schools funded equally,
- All eligible children receive Cradle to Classroom, First Steps, Jet SET, Headstart, Title I, and Pell Grants,
- Fairness in drug sentencing and emphasis on prison rehabilitation.

We must control the media. If you look at military strategy and revolutions, the first thing that the oppressor does is to gain control of the communications industry. One of the major challenges to implementation has been the declining control that Black institutions have over the media. If we wanted to announce tonight through Black media outlets that all of us should send $1 to the United Negro College Fund, Matah, or the National Black Independent Political Party, could we reach 36 million African Americans?

In the early and mid-1900s, we had more than 400 local newspapers. Many of them had a circulation of more than 100,000. One of the ways that Marcus Garvey and Martin Luther King were able to reach large numbers of African Americans was through the local Black newspapers. Many of them were daily papers.

Today, there are approximately 200 local Black newspapers. Less than five are dailies. Most have a circulation of less than 15,000. Do you subscribe to your local Black newspaper? It is bad enough that Fortune 500 companies don't advertise in Black newspapers, but it's a tragedy when Black businesses and the larger Black community do not support their press.

In the 1960s there was a tremendous increase in the number of Black-owned radio stations. The music of James Brown and Marvin Gaye contained a message. The Black community also benefited from an increase in Black talk radio. With recent FCC decisions allowing media companies to own a greater percentage of outlets in a particular city, there has been a tremendous decline in Black-owned radio stations. In addition, many of the Black stations that have survived are music and not talk oriented. Due to the FCC, there are now Fortune 500 media companies that literally own the major newspaper, one of the major television stations, and numerous radio outlets in the same market. It is no accident that the limited amount of news aired about the Black community is identical on television, radio, and in newspapers.

Even more disappointing is the fact that the larger Black community does not realize it's being confined, limited, and "dumbed" down relative to its exposure to ideas. Nationwide, people often ask me, "What are Jesse Jackson, Sr., Louis Farrakhan, Al Sharpton, and other Black leaders doing?" Part of the problem is that the Black community is so limited in its sources for news.

In this monopoly-dominated industry, it now takes an extra effort for African Americans to receive Africentric news. With the Black Entertainment Television network no longer being Black owned and now only producing 30 minutes per day of news, three new television networks are trying to find their wings: Tony Brown's Urban American Television Network, Willie Gary's Major Broadcasting Cable Network, and Cathy Hughes' Radio and Television One. The Final Call newspaper,

# Implementation/Models
# of Success

however, has been a tremendous success as our only national Black newspaper, with a circulation estimated at 300,000. Tom Pope at Powernomics Radio and Tavis Smiley through the Tom Joyner Morning Show have done a great job keeping us informed.

The Internet provides us with unlimited opportunity to reach our people through such web pages as Black America on the Web, Africana, Black Voices, etc. The challenge is similar to home ownership: only 40 percent of African Americans presently have access to the web.

It has also been difficult for Black organizations to share their messages in national magazines when Fortune 500 companies have bid up the prices for full-page ads in such publications as Ebony or Essence to more than $40,000 per page. I appeal to those magazines to set aside a minimum of one page per issue for presenting the Black agenda.

In my opinion, the four organizations that have the greatest potential to implement the solutions outlined and to move the Black agenda forward are the Black Leadership Forum, Black Leadership Roundtable, the Congressional Black Caucus, and the Congress of National Black Churches.

My first question to them is, What is your offensive plan? Specifically, what is your plan for the 20 percent of African American adults and 50 percent of African American children who live below the poverty line?

Often, I try to act as if I'm from another planet visiting America and I want to understand what is going on in Black America. If I were such a visitor and I watched BET for 24 consecutive hours, the meaningless programming would give me a good understanding why the Black community is in its present state. If you've ever attended the Congressional Black Caucus weekend, you'll also gain a better understanding.

# SOLUTIONS FOR BLACK AMERICA

There are plenty of dinners and parties. The Black Leadership Roundtable, led by Rev. Walter Fauntroy, and the Congress of National Black Churches also need much fiscal, financial, and human support.

The most solvent of the four organizations is the Black Leadership Forum. It was founded in 1977 in Washington, DC, as a confederation of civil rights and service organizations, which include the National Urban League, National Urban Coalition, NAACP, SCLC, Joint Center for Political and Economic Studies, the National Council of Negro Women, the NAACP Legal Defense and Educational Fund, the Martin Luther King Center for Nonviolent Social Change, the Congressional Black Caucus, the National Conference of Black Mayors, and the National Business League. The Black Leadership Forum has a paid staff and one annual fund-raiser to support the organization. It also utilizes volunteers. My desire is for the Black Leadership Forum to consider the solutions presented above, in particular that our largest 150 Black organizations refrain from meeting for one year, thus saving $16 billion, to build four regional hotels and acquire a fleet of corporate jets for subsequent years' conferences. In the meantime, every organization should meet in Miami at the Royal Palm Crowne Plaza or Black colleges or churches and consider the solutions provided. I commend Tavis Smiley for hosting the State of the Black Family conference at the Plaza and New Birth Baptist Church.

We often speak about our ancestors who built pyramids 5,000 years ago, that remain as the only one of the seven wonders of the world still standing. The challenge for African Americans in this new millennium, where are the new pyramids and wonders of the world that we built?

In closing, I pray this book has been helpful. To God be the glory!

200

# REFERENCES

1. Woodson, Robert. The Triumphs of Joseph (New York: The Free Press, 1998), p. 12.
2. U.S. Statistical Abstract 2003.
3. Equal Opportunity Journal. August 2003, pp. 75-77.
4. Wilson, Julius. The Truly Disadvantaged (Chicago: University of Chicago Press, 1987), p. 13.
5. Kunjufu, Jawanza. Black Students—Middle-Class Teachers (Chicago: African American Images, 2002), pp. 146-147.
6. Anderson, Claud. Black Labor White Wealth (Maryland: Powernomics Corporation, 1994), p. 25.
7. Carmichael, Stokely. Ready for Revolution (New York: Scribner, 2003), pp. 534-535.
8. T'Shaka, Oba. The Art of Leadership, vol. I (California: Pan Afrikan Publications, 1990), pp. 86-87.
9. Wilson, Amos. Blueprint for Black Power (New York: Afrikan World Infosystems, 1998), p. 442.
10. op. cit., Kunjufu, pp. vi-viii.
11. Penn-Nabrit, Paula. Morning by Morning (New York: Villard Books, 2003), p. 257.
12. Ali, Shahrazad. How to Tell If Your Man Is Gay or Bisexual (Philadelphia: Civilized Publications, 2003), pp. 91-93.
13. Kunjufu, Jawanza. Black Economics, 2nd ed. (Chicago: African American Images, 2003), passim.
14. ibid., passim.
15. Odom, John. Saving Black America (Chicago: African American Images, 2001), pp. 51-53.

16. Anderson, Claud. Powernomics (Maryland: Powernomics Corporation, 2001), p. 130.
17. op. cit., Anderson, Black Labor, White Wealth, p. 133.
18. Winbush, Raymond. Should America Pay? (New York: Amistad, 2003), p. xvi.
19. op. cit., Anderson, Black Labor, White Wealth, p. 35.
20. Sharpton, Al. Al on America (New York: Kensington, 2002), pp. 176-177.
21. op. cit., T'Shaka, p. 27.
22. ibid. p. 53.
23. op. cit., Carmichael, pp. 677-678.
24. Smith, Robert. We Have No Leaders (Albany: New York University Press, 1996), p. 278.
25. Hilliard, Asa. The Maroon Within Us (Baltimore: Black Classic Press, 1995), pp. 71-73.
26. Cross, William. Shades of Black (Philadelphia: Temple University Press, 1991), pp. 164-166.
27. Latif, Sultan and Naimah. Slavery: The African American Psychic Trauma (Chicago: Latif Communications, 1994), pp. 22-25.
28. op. cit., Woodson, p. 12.
29. ibid., pp. 46-48.

# SUBJECT INDEX

# EPILOGUE

More than just a shrewd observer of the early American Asian immigrant, Marcus Garvey, the 1920s African nationalist, pointed out his Asian counterpart as a demonstration to his race of what is possible:

> No sooner does he place his foot upon this soil than he begins to work. No position is too menial, no task is too trivial. He has come to make money, his needs are few. He barely lives, but he saves what he gets. He commences trade in the smallest possible way, and he continually adds to his lot. Others scorn drudgery and remain poor, this newcomer toils patiently, and grows rich. A few years pass by, and he secures warehouses; becomes a contractor for produce; buys foreign goods and employs his newly imported countrymen, who have come to seek their fortune as he did. He is not particularly scrupulous in matters of opinion. He never meddles with politics, for they are dangerous and not profitable. He holds his own with other groups, and works while they sleep. He is diligent, temperate, and uncomplaining. He keeps the word he pledges, pays his debts, and is capable of noble and generous acts. Speak lightly of him if you would speak at all.

"Black America has been led to believe that it has absolutely no power over its economic future," says Henry Parks. "We overemphasize the power of racism and discrimination, and downplay our potential and freedom of choice. The formula has been laid bare: Ethnic price and hard work lead to wealth and success."